Favourite

Muffins, Biscuits, Cakes and Slices

R&R

R&R PUBLICATIONS MARKETING PTY LTD

Published by:
R&R Publications Marketing Pty Ltd
ABN 78 348 105 138
PO Box 254, Carlton North, Victoria 3054 Australia
Phone (61 3) 9381 2199 Fax (61 3) 9381 2689
E-mail: info@randrpublications.com.au
Website: www.randrpublications.com.au
Australia-wide toll-free: 1800 063 296

©Anthony Carroll

Favourite Muffins, Biscuits, Cakes and Slices

Publisher: Anthony Carroll
Cover Designer: Aisling Gallagher
Production Manager: Neil Hargreaves
Food Photography: Robert Monro, Warren Webb, Andrew Warn, William Meppem,
Andrew Elton, Quentin Bacon, Gary Smith, Per Ericson, Steve Baxter, Phillip
Wilkins, David Munns, Thomas Odulate, Christine Hanscomb and Frank Wieder
Food Stylists: Ann Fayle, Susan Bell, Coty Hahn, Janet Lodge, Di Kirby, Helen Payne,
Sue Russell, Sam Scott, Antonia Gaunt and Oded Schwartz
Proofreader: Paul Hassing

ISBN 978-1-74022-652-3

Printed July 2009
Computer Typeset in Futura

Printed in Singapore

Contents

Muffins and Slices Introduction   6

Muffins   10

Slices   34

Quick Bakes   56

Biscuits and Cakes Introduction   78

Biscuit Barrel   84

Chocolate Sensations   114

A Piece of Cake   128

Glossary   152

Weights and Measures   156

Index   158

Muffins and Slices

Nothing beats the taste of home-baked cakes and biscuits. Yet today, many people think of these goodies as nothing more than a delightful memory.

This need not be so. This book will show that baking is not only an easy and affordable way to fill lunch boxes and provide snacks for your family, it's also fun.

Here you'll find a host of easy to make recipes that will bring those distant memories of freshly baked treats back to life. Baking has never been simpler or more fun than with this selection of quick and easy cakes and bakes. A bowl, a beater and a few minutes in the kitchen is all it takes to fill the house with the homey warmth and aroma that only a homemade muffin, cake or batch of biscuits can provide. There's a recipe in these pages to please everyone and every occasion. So, discover the pleasure of home baking and watch your friends and family return for more.

Baking secrets

When adding fresh fruit to batter it's best to follow the following advice: Whole berries and chopped fresh fruit are less likely to sink to the bottom of muffins and other quick breads during baking if you dredge them in flour first. Then shake off the excess flour in a colander before adding them to the batter. Besides helping to suspend the fruit evenly throughout the batter, the flour coating stops moist pieces of fruit from clumping together.

The basic ingredients in muffins – flour, flavourings, perhaps some leavening, and liquid – are the same ones used in almost a dozen other varieties of quick breads. Creating such amazing diversity from a few common staples is largely a matter of adjusting the proportions of dry and liquid ingredients. Use two parts dry to one part liquid ingredients and you get a thicker batter for baking muffins or loaves. Thicker still, with a ratio of dry to liquid ingredients approaching three to one, are soft doughs for cut biscuits and scones.

Muffins and most quick breads are best eaten soon after baking. Those that contain fruit, nuts, vegetables or moderately high amounts of fat stay moist longer than those low in fat. If muffins are left over, it's best to place them in the freezer in an airtight container, where they'll keep for up to 12 months. To reheat, bake the frozen muffins, wrapped in foil, at 175°C for 15–20 minutes, or until heated through. You can also store quick breads and biscuits in the same way.

An accurate oven is essential for successful baking. It should be well insulated and draught-proof, as a discrepancy of a few degrees can ruin baked goods. Regular checking with an oven thermometer helps avoid baking failures.

Muffins

The perfect muffin has a gently rounded top, a golden crust, a moist finely-grained crumb, an appealing aroma and a satisfying balance of flavour. Muffins are mini-cakes for busy home bakers. Freeze them for brunch treats, quick snacks and school lunch boxes, or when you need to stop and take a well-earned break.

Sweet Corn and Cheese Muffins

250g self-raising flour
$\frac{1}{2}$ teaspoon salt
315g can sweet corn kernels, drained
60g cheddar cheese, grated
2 tablespoons grated Parmesan cheese
1 egg, lightly beaten
185mL milk
45g butter, melted

1 Sift flour and salt together in a bowl. Mix in sweet corn, cheddar cheese and Parmesan cheese. Make a well in the centre of the dry ingredients.

2 Place egg, milk and butter in a small bowl and whisk to combine. Pour milk mixture into dry ingredients and mix with a fork until ingredients are just combined.

3 Spoon mixture into 10 greased 250mL capacity muffin tins. Bake for 20–30 minutes or until muffins are cooked when tested with a skewer. Turn onto wire racks to cool.

Makes 10

Oven temperature 180°C, 350°F, Gas 4

Classic Blueberry Muffins

315g self-raising flour
1 teaspoon baking powder
90g sugar
2 eggs, lightly beaten
1 cup buttermilk or milk
60g butter, melted
125g blueberries
2 tablespoons coffee sugar crystals*

1 Sift flour and baking powder together into a bowl, add sugar and mix to combine.

2 Combine eggs, milk and butter. Add egg mixture and blueberries to dry ingredients and mix until just combined.

3 Spoon mixture into 6 greased 250mL capacity muffin tins. Sprinkle with coffee sugar crystals and bake for 20–30 minutes or until muffins are cooked when tested with a skewer. Turn onto wire racks to cool.

Makes 6

Note: *Finely shredded orange rind can be added to this mixture to enhance the flavour of the blueberries.*

*Coffee sugar crystals are coarse golden brown sugar grains. If unavailable, raw (muscovado) or demerara sugar can be used instead.

Oven temperature 200°C, 400°F, Gas 6

Oatbran and Fruit Muffins

180g self-raising flour
30g oat bran
75g brown sugar
½ cup canola oil
2 eggs
125g dried fruit medley
1 cup buttermilk

1 Combine flour, oat, bran and brown sugar. Beat oil and eggs together and stir in the dry ingredients along with the fruit medley and buttermilk. Mix until just combined, do not over mix.

2 Spoon mixture onto lightly greased muffin pans. Bake in an oven at 190°C for 25–30 minutes.

Makes 12

Oven temperature 190°C, 370°F, Gas 5

Mini Sardine Muffins

180g self-raising flour
1 tablespoon lemon thyme
pinch paprika
1 egg
60mL canola oil
180mL milk
125g can sardines in tomato sauce, mashed

1   Combine flour, lemon thyme and paprika in a bowl. In a separate dish mix together the egg, oil and milk. Quickly and lightly combine the dry and liquid ingredients, then fold in the sardines.

2   Spoon mixture into lightly greased muffin pans or patty pans. Bake in an oven at 200°C for 12–14 minutes or until golden. Serve warm.

Makes 24

Oven temperature 200°C, 400°F, Gas 6

Tuna Puffs

2 eggs
60mL cream
1 bunch dill
black pepper to taste
30g Edam cheese, grated
185g can tuna, drained and flaked

1 Beat together the eggs and cream, season to taste with dill and black pepper. Fold in the cheese and tuna.

2 Place spoonfuls of the mixture into lightly greased muffin pans or patty pans.

3 Bake in an oven at 200°C for 10–12 minutes or until puffed and golden. Serve hot or warm.

Makes 12

Oven temperature 200°C, 400°F, Gas 6

Apricot Oatbran Muffins

250g self-raising flour
1 teaspoon baking powder
45g oat bran
60g dried apricots, chopped
60g sultanas
1 egg, lightly beaten
325mL buttermilk or milk
60mL golden syrup
90g butter, melted

1 Sift flour and baking powder together into a bowl. Add oat bran, apricots and sultanas, mix to combine and set aside.
2 Combine egg, milk, golden syrup and butter.
3 Add milk mixture to dry ingredients and mix until just combined. Spoon mixture into 6 greased 250mL capacity muffin tins and bake for 15–20 minutes or until muffins are cooked when tested with a skewer. Serve hot, warm or cold.

Makes 6

Note: Serve this muffin for breakfast or brunch fresh and warm from the oven, split and buttered and perhaps with a drizzle of honey.

Oven temperature 180°C, 350°F, Gas 4

Cornbread Muffins

185g self-raising flour
170g cornmeal (polenta)
45g grated Parmesan cheese
1 teaspoon baking powder
1 teaspoon ground cumin
pinch chilli powder
2 cups buttermilk or low-fat milk
2 eggs, lightly beaten
1 tablespoon polyunsaturated
vegetable oil

1 Place flour, cornmeal (polenta), Parmesan cheese, baking powder, cumin and chilli powder in a bowl and mix to combine.
2 Make a well in the centre of the flour mixture, add milk, eggs and oil and mix until just combined.
3 Spoon mixture into 12 greased 90mL muffin tins and bake for 30 minutes or until muffins are cooked when tested with a skewer.

Makes 12

Note: Cornmeal (polenta) is cooked yellow maize flour and is very popular in northern Italian and southern American cooking. It adds an interesting texture and flavour to baked products such as these muffins and is available from health-food stores and some supermarkets.

Oven temperature 190°C, 375°F, Gas 5

Choc-Rough Muffins Photograph opposite

125g butter, softened
125g sugar
2 eggs, lightly beaten
250g self-raising flour, sifted
30g cocoa powder, sifted
155g chocolate chips
45g shredded coconut
185mL buttermilk or milk

1 Place butter and sugar in a bowl and beat until light and fluffy. Gradually beat in eggs.

2 Combine flour and cocoa powder. Add the flour mixture, chocolate chips, coconut and milk to the butter mixture and mix until just combined.

3 Spoon mixture into 6 greased 250mL capacity muffin tins and bake for 35 minutes or until muffins are cooked when tested with a skewer.

Makes 6

Note: Muffin tins without a non-stick finish should be greased (and, if desired, lined with paper baking cups) before use. Non-stick tins do not need lining but may need greasing; follow the manufacturer's instructions.

Oven temperature 180°C, 350°F, Gas 4

Cheesy Apple Muffins

165g wholemeal self-raising flour
1/4 teaspoon ground cinnamon
1/4 teaspoon ground nutmeg
1/4 teaspoon ground ginger
1/4 teaspoon ground cloves
1 teaspoon baking powder
45g oatbran
3 tablespoons brown sugar
1 green apple, peeled and grated
125g ricotta cheese
2 tablespoons polyunsaturated oil
180mL apple juice

1 Sift flour, cinnamon, nutmeg, ginger, cloves and baking powder into a mixing bowl. Add oatbran and sugar.

2 Make a well in the centre of the flour mixture. Stir in the apple, ricotta, oil and apple juice. Mix until just combined. Spoon the mixture into lightly greased muffin pans.

3 Bake at 200°C for 25 minutes or until golden brown.

Makes 12

Oven temperature 200°C, 400°F, Gas 6

Mushroom Muffins

250g plain flour
1 tablespoon baking powder
60g fresh mushrooms, chopped
75g cooked brown rice
60g shredded tasty cheese
1 tablespoon parsley flakes
2 teaspoons chives, chopped
125g margarine, melted
1 cup milk
1 egg, beaten

1 Sift flour and baking powder into a large bowl. Mix in mushrooms, rice, cheese and herbs.

2 Make a well in the centre of the dry ingredients. Add the remaining ingredients. Mix until just combined (see note).

3 Spoon the mixture into greased muffin tins until ¾ full. Bake in the oven at 200°C for 25 minutes. Remove from the tin. Cool on a wire rack. Serve hot or cold.

Makes about 12

Note: Don't worry if not all the flour is incorporated as this gives muffins their characteristic texture. 16 strokes is usually enough when mixing.

Oven temperature 200°C, 400°F, Gas 6

Banana Choc-Chip Muffins

1 large ripe banana
1 cup milk
1 egg
60g margarine, melted
180g self-raising flour
125g caster sugar
125g choc bits

1 In a mixing bowl mash the banana and add the milk, egg and margarine. Mix well.

2 Stir the flour, sugar and choc bits into the banana mixture, mixing only until the ingredients are combined.

3 Spoon the mixture into well greased muffin tins. Bake in an oven at 190°C for 20 minutes. Serve warm or cold.

Makes 12

Oven temperature 190°C, 370°F, Gas 5

Blackberry Spice Muffins Photograph opposite

75g self-raising wholemeal flour
60g self-raising flour
½ teaspoon ground allspice
45g brown sugar
60g ground almonds
185g blackberries
1 banana, mashed
1 cup buttermilk
90mL vegetable oil
1 egg, lightly beaten

1 Sift together wholemeal flour, flour and allspice into a bowl. Return husks to bowl. Add sugar, almonds, blackberries and banana and mix to combine.

2 Place buttermilk, oil and egg in a bowl and whisk to combine. Stir milk mixture into dry ingredients and mix until just combined.

3 Spoon mixture into 12 non-stick 125mL capacity muffin tins and bake for 15–20 minutes or until muffins are cooked when tested with a skewer. Turn onto a wire rack to cool.

Makes 12

Note: If buttermilk is unavailable, use equal parts of low-fat natural yoghurt and reduced-fat milk instead.

Oven temperature 190°C, 375°F, Gas 5

Mango Bran Muffins Photograph opposite

125g self-raising flour
2 teaspoons baking powder
1 teaspoon ground cardamom
45g oatbran
60g brown sugar
1 mango, chopped
2 egg whites
185mL reduced-fat milk
60mL vegetable oil

1 Sift together flour, baking powder and cardamom into a bowl. Add oatbran, sugar and mango and mix to combine.

2 Place egg whites, milk and oil in a bowl and whisk to combine. Stir milk mixture into flour mixture and mix well to combine.

3 Spoon mixture into 12 non-stick 90mL capacity muffin tins and bake for 15–20 minutes or until muffins are cooked when tested with a skewer. Turn onto a wire rack to cool.

Makes 12

Note: When fresh mangoes are unavailable, drained, canned mangoes can be used instead.

Oven temperature 190°C, 375°F, Gas 5

Apple and Bran Muffins

230g wholemeal self-raising flour
¹/₂ teaspoon ground nutmeg
¹/₄ teaspoon baking powder
30g bran cereal, toasted
60g brown sugar
2 green apples, grated
2 eggs, lightly beaten
45g low-fat natural yoghurt
1 tablespoon polyunsaturated vegetable oil

1 Sift together flour, nutmeg and baking powder into a bowl. Add bran cereal and sugar and mix to combine.

2 Make a well in the centre of the flour mixture. Add apples, eggs, yoghurt and oil and mix until just combined.

3 Spoon mixture into 12 greased 125mL muffin tins and bake for 15 minutes or until muffins are cooked when tested with a skewer.

Makes 12

Note: The secret to making great muffins is in the mixing – they should be mixed as little as possible. While it doesn't matter if the mixture is lumpy, overmixing results in tough muffins.

Oven temperature 180°C, 350°F, Gas 4

Lemon-Poppy Seed Muffins

2 eggs, lightly beaten
$^1/_2$ cup sour cream
$^1/_2$ cup milk
60mL olive oil
90mL honey
3 tablespoons poppy seeds
1 tablespoon grated lemon rind
280g self-raising flour, sifted

Lemon Cream-Cheese Icing
60g cream cheese, softened
1 tablespoon lemon juice
125g icing sugar

Muffins

1 Place eggs, sour cream, milk, oil, honey, poppy seeds and lemon rind in a bowl and mix well to combine.

2 Add flour to poppy seed mixture and mix until just combined.

3 Spoon mixture into six greased 250mL capacity muffin tins and bake for 25–30 minutes or until muffins are cooked when tested with a skewer. Turn onto wire racks to cool.

Lemon Cream-Cheese Icing

1 Place cream cheese, lemon juice and icing sugar in a food processor and process until smooth. Top cold muffins with icing.

Makes 6

Note: A simple glacé icing is another suitable topping for muffins. To make, sift 155g icing sugar into a bowl, slowly stir in 3 teaspoons of warm water and a few drops of almond or vanilla essence to make a glaze of drizzling consistency. To vary the flavour, omit the essence and substitute the water with 3 teaspoons of citrus juice or a favourite liqueur.

Oven temperature 180°C, 350°F, Gas 4

Banana and Pineapple Muffins Photograph opposite

165g wholemeal self-raising flour
1 teaspoon baking powder
1 teaspoon mixed spice
4 tablespoons brown sugar
45g oatbran
1 small banana, mashed
150g canned crushed
pineapple, drained
3 egg whites, lightly beaten
2 tablespoons polyunsaturated oil
$\frac{1}{2}$ cup pineapple juice

1 Sift flour, baking powder and spice into a mixing bowl. Add sugar and oatbran.
2 Make a well in the centre of the dry ingredients. Combine the banana, pineapple, egg whites, oil and juice. Stir into the flour mixture and mix to combine all ingredients.
3 Spoon mixture into lightly greased muffin pans. Bake at 200°C for 12–15 minutes or until golden brown.

Makes 12

Oven temperature 200°C, 400°F, Gas 6

Orange and Blueberry Muffins

1 orange
$\frac{1}{2}$ cup orange juice
125g butter, chopped
1 egg
185g plain flour
170g caster sugar
1 teaspoon bicarbonate of soda
1 teaspoon baking powder
$\frac{1}{4}$ teaspoon salt
125g frozen or fresh blueberries

1 Preheat oven to 200°C. Peel the rind from the orange, remove all pith, and cut the rind into small pieces. Remove membrane and seeds from orange and cut the orange into segments.
2 Place orange rind and segments, orange juice, butter and egg in a food processor and process until well combined (mixture will curdle). Transfer mixture to a large bowl.
3 Sift together flour, sugar, bicarbonate of soda, baking powder and salt, add to orange mixture and lightly mix. Batter should be lumpy. Fold in the berries.
4 Divide batter between 12–16 greased 90mL capacity muffin tins, filling $\frac{2}{3}$ full. Bake for 18–20 minutes until cooked and golden. Cool on wire racks.

Makes 12–16

Oven temperature 200°C, 400°F, Gas 6

Potato Sour-Cream Muffins Photograph opposite

250g mashed potato
2 eggs, lightly beaten
1 cup milk
185g sour cream
60g butter, melted
315g self-raising flour, sifted
3 tablespoons snipped fresh chives

1 Place potato in a bowl. Add eggs, milk, sour cream and butter to the bowl and mix well to combine.

2 Combine flour and chives. Add to potato mixture and mix until just combined. Spoon mixture into 6 greased 250mL capacity muffin tins and bake for 25–30 minutes or until muffins are cooked when tested with a skewer. Serve warm or cold.

Makes 6

Note: A properly cooked muffin should have risen well, be slightly domed in the middle (but not peaked) and be evenly browned. It should also shrink slightly from the sides of the tin.

Oven temperature 180°C, 350°F, Gas 4

Cheese and Bacon Muffins Photograph opposite

4 rashers bacon, chopped
1 egg, lightly beaten
1 cup milk
60mL vegetable oil
2 tablespoons chopped fresh parsley
250g self-raising flour, sifted
90g grated tasty (mature cheddar) cheese

1 Place bacon in a frying pan and cook over a medium heat, stirring, until crisp. Remove bacon from pan and drain on absorbent kitchen paper.

2 Place egg, milk, oil and parsley in a bowl and mix to combine. Combine flour and cheese. Add flour mixture and bacon to egg mixture and mix until combined.

3 Spoon mixture into 12 greased 125mL capacity muffin tins and bake for 20–25 minutes or until muffins are cooked when tested with a skewer. Serve warm or cold.

Makes 12

Note: An accurate oven is essential for successful baking. It should be well insulated and draught-proof, as a discrepancy of a few degrees can ruin baked goods. Regular checking with an oven thermometer helps avoid baking failures.

Oven temperature 180°C, 350°F, Gas 4

Spiced Apple Muffins

200g plain wholemeal flour
1 tablespoon baking powder
1 teaspoon ground mixed spice
pinch of salt
50g light soft brown sugar
1 medium egg, beaten
200mL half-fat milk
50g margarine, melted
1 cooking apple, peeled, cored
and chopped

1. Preheat the oven to 200°C. Line a muffin or deep bun tin with 9 muffin cases and set aside. Place the flour, baking powder, mixed spice and salt in a bowl and mix well.

2. In a separate large bowl, mix together the sugar, egg, milk and margarine, then gently fold in the flour mixture – just enough to combine them. The mixture should look quite lumpy; it will produce heavy muffins if overmixed. Gently fold in the apple.

3. Divide the mixture between the muffin cases. Bake in the oven for 20 minutes or until risen and golden brown. Transfer to a wire rack to cool.

Makes 9

Note: The problem with these muffins is that they smell so good when they come out of the oven, they may not last until tea time! Serve them on their own with a cup of tea.

Oven temperature 200°C, 400°F, Gas 6

Carrot and Sesame Muffins

375g self-raising flour
½ teaspoon bicarbonate of soda
1 teaspoon ground mixed spice
90g brown sugar
1 large carrot, grated
4 tablespoons toasted sesame seeds
170g sultanas
200g natural yoghurt
1 cup milk
3 tablespoons melted butter
3 egg whites, lightly beaten

1 Sift together flour, bicarbonate of soda and mixed spice into a large bowl. Add sugar, carrot, sesame seeds and sultanas and mix to combine.

2 Place yoghurt, milk, butter and egg whites in a bowl and whisk to combine. Stir yoghurt mixture into flour mixture and mix until just combined. Spoon batter into lightly greased muffin tins and bake for 20 minutes or until golden and cooked.

Makes 24

Note: Delicious light muffins are perfect weekend fare. Any leftovers can be frozen and used when time is short.

Oven temperature 200°C, 400°F, Gas 6

Sticky Date Muffins

250g self-raising flour
1 teaspoon bicarbonate of soda
1 teaspoon ground cinnamon
60g brown sugar
90g butter
125g chopped dates
1 egg, lightly beaten
1 cup buttermilk or milk

Brandy Sauce
100g butter
45g brown sugar
1 tablespoon golden syrup
1 tablespoon brandy (optional)

Muffins

1 Sift flour, bicarbonate of soda and cinnamon together into a bowl. Set aside.

2 Place sugar, butter and dates in a saucepan and heat over a low heat, stirring constantly, until butter melts. Pour date mixture into dry ingredients, add egg and milk. Mix until just combined.

3 Spoon mixture into six greased 250mL capacity muffin tins and bake for 30 minutes or until muffins are cooked when tested with a skewer.

Brandy Sauce

1 Place butter, sugar, golden syrup and brandy (if using) in a saucepan and heat over a low heat, stirring constantly, until sugar dissolves. Bring to the boil, then reduce heat and simmer for 3 minutes or until sauce is thick and syrupy. Serve with warm muffins.

Makes 6

Note: If 250mL capacity muffin tins are unavailable, use the standard 125mL capacity tins and bake for approximately half the recommended time. The yield, of course, will be doubled. These muffins make a delicious dessert treat, but are just as good in lunch boxes and for snacks without the sauce.

Oven temperature 190°C, 375°F, Gas 5

Slices

Your family and friends will be delighted when you open a cake tin that actually contains a selection of homemade slices. The recipes in this chapter are great for morning and afternoon teas and are equally good in packed lunches.

Macadamia Caramel Squares

Base
100g white melting chocolate
125g butter
90g icing sugar
60g macadamia nuts, roasted and ground
200g plain flour

Topping
400g can sweetened condensed milk
200g milk chocolate suitable for melting, such as 'melts'
2 large eggs
2 tablespoons plain flour
90g shortbread biscuits chopped, not crushed
200g roasted macadamia nuts roughly chopped
60g roasted macadamia nuts (extra)

Base

1 Preheat oven to 180°C. Butter a lamington tin 28 x 18cm then line it with baking paper.

2 Melt the white chocolate then add it to a mixer with the butter, icing sugar, crushed macadamia nuts and plain flour.

3 Mix on low speed until all the ingredients are combined, then press the mixture into the prepared tin. Bake for 18 minutes, then cool.

Topping

1 Preheat the oven to 160°C. In a saucepan, heat the condensed milk and milk chocolate together (until the chocolate has melted). Add the eggs, flour, shortbread biscuit pieces and chopped macadamia nuts, and mix gently.

2 Pour this mixture over the base, then sprinkle the extra macadamia nuts over. Bake at 160°C for 40 minutes. Remove from the oven and cool completely in the refrigerator before slicing.

Makes 18

Note: This delicious confection will be adored by adults and children alike. A sure winner for picnics and outdoor entertaining, the brownie-like consistency will keep them coming back for more!

Oven temperature 160°C, 325°F, Gas 3

Lamingtons (Microwave)

175g butter
180g caster sugar
3 eggs
180g self-raising flour
½ teaspoon baking powder
4 tablespoons milk

Chocolate Icing
465g icing sugar
3 tablespoons cocoa
2 tablespoons butter
5 tablespoons water
180g coconut, dessicated

Lamingtons

1 Cream butter and sugar together, add egg and beat well. Sift flour and baking powder together, stir into mixture alternately with milk.

2 Pour into a lightly greased 28 x 18cm, or 22cm square microwave dish.

3 Elevate and cook on power level 9 (High) for 7 minutes.

4 Allow to stand for 10 minutes then turn out and allow to cool completely and trim the sides. Cut into 12 even pieces.

Chocolate Icing

1 Place all ingredients except the coconut into a large bowl. Heat on power level 9 (High) for 3 minutes.

2 Stir after 1 minute; at this stage mixture will be stiff, but on further heating it will come to a pouring consistency.

3 Spread coconut onto a sheet of paper. Working quickly, dip cakes one a time into icing, turn to coat both sides, then remove with a fork. Drain off excess icing and toss in coconut.

4 Icing will cool and stiffen after 3 or 4 lamingtons are dipped. Just return to microwave and heat for 20 seconds on high. Repeat process until all 12 are completed.

Makes 12

Hint: To ice party cakes quickly, dip the top of each cake into soft icing, twirl slightly and quickly turn right side up.

Microwave temp: Level 9 (High)

Hot Brownies with White Chocolate Sauce

100g soft margarine, plus extra
for greasing
100g soft dark brown sugar
1 large egg, beaten
1 tablespoon golden syrup
1 tablespoon cocoa powder, sifted
50g wholemeal self-raising flour, sifted
25g pecan nuts or walnuts, chopped

White Chocolate Sauce
1 tablespoon cornflour
200mL full-fat milk
50g white chocolate, broken into
small chunks

Brownies

1   Preheat the oven to 180°C. Grease the sides and base of
    an 18cm square cake tin. Beat the margarine and sugar in
    a bowl until pale and creamy, then beat in the egg, syrup,
    cocoa powder and flour until it forms a thick, smooth batter.
    Stir in the nuts.

2   Spoon the mixture into the tin, smooth the top and bake for
    35–40 minutes, until well risen and just firm to the touch.

White Chocolate Sauce

1   Meanwhile, make the chocolate sauce. Blend the cornflour
    with 1 tablespoon of the milk. Heat the rest of the milk in
    a saucepan, add the cornflour mixture, then gently bring to
    the boil, stirring as the sauce thickens. Cook gently for 1–2
    minutes.

2   Add the white chocolate, then remove from the heat and stir
    until it melts. Cut the brownies into 8 pieces and serve warm
    with the chocolate sauce.

*Note: These brownies are delicious cold, but served straight from the
oven with white chocolate sauce spooned over them, they're absolutely
fabulous!*

Oven temperature 180°C, 350°F, Gas 4

Fruit Slice

Base
180g self-raising flour
2¹/₂ tablespoon cornflour
60g ground rice
250g butter or margarine
60g caster sugar
1 egg

Filling
250g dates, chopped
125g sultanas
125g raisins
30g mixed peel
30g glace cherries
1 tablespoon butter or margarine
mixed spice, to taste
170g can passionfruit pulp
1 tablespoon arrowroot
2 tablespoons water
beaten egg and caster sugar
for glazing

Base

1 Sift the flours into a bowl and stir in the ground rice.

2 Rub in the butter or margarine, stir in the sugar and bind together with the egg. Press half the mixture over the base of a buttered and lined lamington tin.

Filling

1 Combine the fruit, butter or margarine, spice and passionfruit in a saucepan and stir over a low heat until the mixture thickens slightly. Blend the arrowroot and water together, stir into the fruit and allow to cook, stirring all the time for 3 minutes.

2 Remove from the heat and cool. Spoon the filling onto the pastry base and top with the remaining pastry, crimping the edges to decorate and seal. Glaze with the beaten egg, sprinkle with sugar and bake at 220°C for 20–25 minutes. Serve warm with custard.

Serves 8–10

Oven temperature 220°C, 440°F, Gas 7

Brandy Apricot Slice

90g dried apricots, chopped
2 tablespoons brandy
100g dark chocolate
4 tablespoons margarine
3 tablespoons milk
1 egg
60g caster sugar
90g plain flour
¼ teaspoon baking powder

Chocolate Frosting
60g dark chocolate
1 tablespoon milk
250g sifted icing sugar
1 tablespoon margarine

1 Combine apricots and brandy. Set aside for 15 minutes. Sieve the flour. Melt chocolate and margarine together, stir in milk, egg, sugar and the sifted flour and baking powder. Mix well. Stir apricots through the chocolate mixture.

2 Spoon mixture into a lightly greased 20cm square sandwich pan. Bake in an oven at 180°C for 12–15 minutes or until firm. Cool in the tin. Ice with chocolate frosting.

Chocolate Frosting

1 Melt together chocolate and milk, and blend in icing sugar and margarine. Mix well.

Makes 16

Oven temperature 180°C, 350°F, Gas 4

Sticky Chocolate and Raspberry Slice

75g unsalted butter, plus extra
for greasing
75g plain chocolate, broken
into chunks
75g fresh or frozen raspberries, plus
extra to decorate
2 medium eggs, separated
50g caster sugar
25g ground almonds
25g cocoa powder, sifted
25g plain flour,
sifted icing sugar to dust and fresh
mint to decorate

Raspberry Sauce
150g fresh or frozen raspberries
1 tablespoon caster sugar (optional)

1   Preheat the oven to180°C. Grease the base and sides of an
    18cm loose-bottomed cake tin and line with baking paper.
    Melt the butter and chocolate in a bowl set over a saucepan
    of simmering water, stirring. Cool slightly.

2   Press the raspberries through a sieve. Whisk the egg yolks and
    sugar until pale and creamy, then mix in the almonds, cocoa,
    flour, melted chocolate and sieved raspberries.

3   Whisk the egg whites until they form stiff peaks (this is best
    done with an electric whisk). Fold a little into the chocolate
    mixture to loosen, then fold in the remainder. Spoon into the tin
    and cook for 25 minutes or until risen and just firm. Cool for 1
    hour.

4   Remove the cake from the tin and dust with the icing sugar.
    Serve with the sauce, decorated with mint and raspberries.

Raspberry Sauce

1   Sieve the raspberries, then stir in the sugar, if using.

Oven temperature 180°C, 350°F, Gas 4

Chocolate Pecan Fingers

90g dark chocolate
125g margarine
2 teaspoons instant coffee powder
2 eggs
180g caster sugar
½ teaspoon vanilla
125g plain flour
90g chopped pecans
icing sugar, for dusting

1 Melt the chocolate and margarine together over hot water, stir in the coffee powder and allow to cool slightly.

2 In a medium sized bowl whisk the eggs until foamy, add the sugar and vanilla.

3 Fold the chocolate mixture through the eggs. Stir in the flour and pecans and mix until just blended. Spoon the mixture into a lightly greased 20cm square cake pan. Bake in an oven at 180°C for 25 minutes or until the cake springs back when touched. Cool in the tin. Dust with sifted icing sugar and cut into fingers to serve.

Makes about 15

Oven temperature 180°C, 350°F, Gas 4

Sultana Oat Slice

4 tablespoons margarine
75mL honey
1 packet sultana buttercake
2 eggs
30g rolled oats

Yoghurt Frosting
300g icing sugar, sifted
2 tablespoons vanilla yoghurt
4 tablespoons toasted shredded coconut

1   In a small saucepan melt the margarine and honey together. Combine the sultana buttercake, eggs and rolled oats, pour the melted ingredients over the buttercake mixture and mix well.

2   Spoon mixture into a lightly greased 20cm square sandwich tin. Bake in an oven at 180°C for 20 minutes or until firm to the touch. Cool before icing with yoghurt frosting, sprinkle with toasted shredded coconut. Cut into squares to serve.

Yoghurt Frosting

1   Mix sugar and vanilla and beat until smooth.

Makes 16 slices

45

Pistachio Truffles

315g dark chocolate, broken into pieces
45g butter, chopped
1/2 cup thickened double cream
2 tablespoons sugar
2 tablespoons Galliano liqueur
125g chopped pistachio nuts

1 Place chocolate, butter, cream and sugar in a heatproof bowl set over a saucepan of simmering water and heat, stirring, until mixture is smooth. Add liqueur and half the pistachio nuts and mix well to combine. Chill the mixture for 1 hour or until firm enough to roll into balls.

2 Roll tablespoons of the mixture into balls, then roll the balls in the remaining pistachio nuts. Chill until required.

Serves 4

Tip: To bring out the bright green colour of the pistachios, blanch the shelled nuts in boiling water for 30 seconds, drain and vigorously rub in a clean towel to remove their skins.

Caramel-Walnut Petits Fours

250g sugar
90g brown sugar
2 cups thickened double cream
1 cup golden syrup
60g butter, chopped
1/2 teaspoon bicarbonate of soda
155g chopped walnuts
1 tablespoon vanilla essence

Chocolate Icing
375g dark or milk chocolate, melted
2 teaspoons vegetable oil

1 Place sugar, brown sugar, cream, golden syrup and butter in a saucepan and heat over a low heat, stirring constantly, until sugar dissolves. As sugar crystals form on the sides of the pan, brush with a wet pastry brush.

2 Bring the syrup to the boil and stir in the bicarbonate of soda. Reduce heat and simmer until syrup reaches the hard-ball stage or 120°C on a sugar thermometer.

3 Stir in walnuts and vanilla essence and pour mixture into a greased and foil-lined 20cm square cake tin. Set aside at room temperature for 5 hours or until caramel sets.

4 Remove caramel from the tin and cut into 2cm squares.

Chocolate Icing

1 Combine chocolate and oil. Half dip caramels in melted chocolate, place on greaseproof paper and leave to set.

Makes 40

Note: To easily remove the caramel from the tin, let the foil lining overhang the tin on two opposite sides to form handles for lifting.

Fruit Medley Slice

100g margarine
125g self-raising flour
155g brown sugar
90g desiccated coconut

Topping
250g dried fruit medley
4 tablespoons orange juice
155g brown sugar
6 tablespoons margarine, melted
60g chopped pecans
45g desiccated coconut
100g white chocolate, melted

1 Combine the margarine, flour, brown sugar and coconut. Mix well. Press mixture onto the base of a 30 x 20cm slice tin.

2 Bake in an oven at 180°C for 15 minutes. Remove from the oven and pour the topping over the base. Then return to the oven and cook for a further 15 minutes. Cool in the tin.

3 Decorate top with melted chocolate and cut into squares to serve.

Topping

1 Soak fruit medley in orange juice for 10 minutes. Combine with brown sugar, melted margarine, pecans and coconut. Mix well.

Tip: Keep icing in a bowl covered with a damp cloth to prevent it from drying out and forming a crust.

Oven temperature 180°C, 350°F, Gas 4

Baklava

250g unsalted butter, melted

400g blanched roasted almonds, ground

1½ teaspoons cinnamon

½ cup caster sugar

700g filo pastry

Syrup

3 cups caster sugar

1½ cups water

1 cinnamon stick

1 piece of orange or lemon rind

1 tablespoon honey

1. Melt butter, set aside.
2. Mix nuts in a bowl, add cinnamon and sugar.
3. Brush a 25 x 33cm baking tray with the butter. Place 1 sheet of filo on the bottom of the dish with ends hanging over sides. Brush with melted butter and add another layer of filo. Repeat with 8 more filo sheets.
4. Sprinkle nut mixture generously over the filo. Continue the layering of filo pastry (3 sheets) and 1 layer of nuts until all the nuts are used.
5. Top with 8 reserved sheets of filo, making sure the top sheet is well buttered. Cut the top lengthways in parallel strips.
6. Bake in an oven at 180°C for 30 minutes, then reduce the heat to 150°C and bake for a further hour. Pour cold syrup over the baklava and cut it into diamond shapes.

Syrup

1. Place ingredients in saucepan and bring to the boil. Reduce heat and let simmer for 10–15 minutes. Leave to cool before use.

Two-Fruit Crumble Slice

Base
125g sweet biscuits
125g butter
125g brown sugar
100g milk chocolate (suitable for melting, such as 'melts')
75g desiccated coconut
1 tablespoon cocoa

Filling
250g dried apricots
250g dried peaches
1 tablespoon honey
juice and zest of two oranges
50mL water

Topping
90g shredded coconut
75g rolled oats
90g butter
2 tablespoons golden syrup
60g cashew nuts (salted, roasted and chopped)

Base

1 Preheat oven to 180°C and butter a 20cm square cake tin.
2 Using a food processor, crush the sweet biscuits until finely ground.
3 Place the butter, brown sugar and chocolate in a saucepan and heat gently stirring well to avoid burning. When the mixture has melted, add the coconut, biscuit crumbs and cocoa, and stir vigorously until the mixture is well combined. Press evenly into the base of the prepared cake tin and bake for 10 minutes. Cool.

Filling

1 Chop the dried fruit and place in a saucepan with the honey, orange juice and zest and water, and bring to the boil. Simmer for 10 minutes, until the fruit has softened and all the liquid has been absorbed. Allow to cool, then spread over the cooked biscuit base.

Topping

1 Mix the coconut and oats together, cook in the microwave on 'high' for 2 minutes then stir gently. Cook for a further minute or two until deep golden. In a separate bowl or small saucepan, heat the butter and golden syrup together until bubbling, then stir in the oat mixture and cashews, and mix thoroughly until all ingredients are moistened.
2 Sprinkle the topping over the filling to cover it completely, then bake for a further 15–18 minutes until the topping is golden. Remove from the oven and cool, then slice into 16 even pieces.

Makes 16

Note: One of the best sweet choices when entertaining is a slice— usually a fairly flat, cake mixture that has two or three layers of different flavours and textures. Slices are usually made well ahead of time, allowing the cook to enjoy socialising as much as the guests do. Most slices travel well, making them perfect for gifts, picnics and school lunches.

Oven temperature 180°C, 350°F, Gas 4

Strawberry and Chocolate Slice

250g chocolate biscuits
3 tablespoons butter
1 tablespoon gelatine
60mL water
250g packet cream cheese
300mL thickened cream
150g packet marshmallows
1 punnet strawberries

1   Line a 28 x18cm lamington tin with plastic wrap.

2   Place biscuits into a food processor and process until fine. Combine with melted butter and press into the base of the tin, refrigerate until firm.

3   Sprinkle the gelatine over the water, dissolve over hot water, allow to cool.

4   Place cream cheese into a food processor and process until smooth. Add the cream, gelatine, marshmallows and half the strawberries and process until well mixed.

5   Pour the filling over the biscuit base and decorate with the remaining halved strawberries, chill until firm. Remove the slice from the pan and cut into slices to serve.

Makes 12

Chocolate Panforte

1 cup liquid honey
250g sugar
250g almonds, toasted and chopped
250g hazelnuts, toasted and chopped
125g glacé apricots, chopped
125g glacé peaches, chopped
100g candied mixed peel
185g flour, sifted
45g cocoa powder, sifted
2 teaspoons ground cinnamon
155g dark chocolate, melted
rice paper

1 Place honey and sugar in a small saucepan and heat, stirring constantly, over a low heat until the sugar dissolves. Bring to the boil, then reduce the heat and simmer, stirring constantly, for 5 minutes or until mixture thickens.

2 Place almonds, hazelnuts, apricots, peaches, mixed peel, flour, cocoa powder and cinnamon in a bowl and mix to combine. Stir in the honey syrup. Add the chocolate and mix well to combine.

3 Line a shallow 18 x 28cm cake tin with rice paper. Pour the mixture into the tin and bake for 20 minutes. Turn onto a wire rack to cool, then cut into small pieces.

Makes 32

Note: Everyone's favourite biscuits is full of the flavour, of fruit, toasted almonds, hazelnuts and a generous portion of chocolate!

Oven temperature 180°C, 350°F, Gas 4

Double-Fudge Blondies

250g butter, softened
375g sugar
1 teaspoon vanilla essence
4 eggs, lightly beaten
225g plain flour
½ teaspoon baking powder
180g white chocolate, melted

Cream Cheese Filling
200g cream cheese, softened
80g white chocolate, melted
2 tablespoons maple syrup
1 egg
1 tablespoon plain flour

Cream Cheese Filling

1 Place cream cheese, chocolate, maple syrup, egg and flour in a bowl and beat until smooth. Set aside.

Blondies

1 Place butter, sugar and vanilla essence in a bowl and beat until light and fluffy. Gradually beat in the eggs.

2 Sift together the flour and baking powder over the butter mixture. Add the chocolate and mix well to combine.

3 Spread half the mixture over the base of a greased and lined 23cm square cake tin. Top with cream cheese filling and then with the remaining mixture. Bake at 180°C for 45 minutes or until firm. Cool in the tin, then cut into squares.

Makes 24

Note: These lusciously rich white brownies can double as a dessert if drizzled with melted white or dark chocolate and topped with toasted flaked almonds.

Oven temperature 180°C, 350°F, Gas 4

Chocolate Nougat Hearts

375g milk chocolate, broken
into pieces
45g butter, chopped
1 cup thickened double cream
200g nougat, chopped
100g almonds, toasted and chopped

1. Place chocolate, butter and cream in a heatproof bowl set over a saucepan of simmering water and heat, stirring, until mixture is smooth.
2. Add nougat and almonds and mix well to combine. Pour mixture into a greased and lined, shallow 18 x 28cm cake tin. Refrigerate for 2 hours or until set.
3. Using a heart-shaped cutter, cut out hearts from the set mixture.

Makes 40

Note: Dip the cutter in warm water and dry on a clean towel between each cut to achieve evenly straight edges.

Quick Bakes

Baking has never been simpler or more fun than with this selection of quick and easy cakes and bakes. A bowl, a beater and few minutes in the kitchen is all it takes to fill the house with the homely warmth and aroma that only a homemade scone or loaf of bread can provide. There's a recipe on these pages to please everyone and every occasion. So, discover the pleasure of home baking and watch your friends and family return for more.

Soda Bread Photograph on Page 56

500g plain flour
1 teaspoon bicarbonate of soda
1 teaspoon salt
45g butter
2 cups buttermilk or milk

1 Sift together the flour, bicarbonate of soda and salt into a bowl. Rub in the butter, using your fingertips, until the mixture resembles coarse breadcrumbs. Make a well in the centre of the flour mixture, pour in the milk or buttermilk and, using a round-ended knife, mix to form a soft dough.

2 Turn dough onto a floured surface and knead lightly until smooth. Shape into an 18cm round and place on a greased and floured baking tray. Score dough into eighths using a sharp knife. Dust lightly with flour and bake for 35–40 minutes or until the loaf sounds hollow when tapped on the base.

Serves 8

Note: A loaf for when you need bread unexpectedly, soda bread is made with bicarbonate of soda rather than yeast so it needs no rising. Its best eaten slightly warm and is delicious with lashings of treacle or golden syrup.

Oven temperature 200°C, 400°F, Gas 6

Fig Scones Photograph on Page 56

250g self-raising flour
65g sugar
3/4 teaspoon salt
125g butter
65g finely chopped dried figs
2 eggs, slightly beaten
milk, for brushing
cinnamon and sugar, for glaze

1 Sift all dry ingredients together. Rub in the butter, add the figs and the egg. Stir with a fork until the mixture forms a soft ball.

2 Roll out onto a lightly floured board about 1cm thick and cut into triangles or rounds. Brush the tops with a little milk, sprinkle with sugar and cinnamon and bake in an oven at 200°C until golden brown, about 15 minutes.

Serves 3–4

Oven temperature 200°C, 400°F, Gas 6

Fresh Strawberry Scones

250g self-raising wholemeal flour
1 teaspoon baking powder
pinch of salt
60g margarine
30g caster sugar
100g fresh strawberries, chopped
100mL half-fat milk, plus extra
for glazing

1 Preheat the oven to 220°C. Put the flour, baking powder and salt in a large bowl and stir to mix. Lightly rub in the margarine until the mixture resembles breadcrumbs.

2 Mix in the sugar and strawberries, then add enough milk to form a soft dough. Turn the dough out onto a floured surface, knead lightly, then carefully roll to a thickness of 2cm.

3 Cut out 12 rounds, using a 5cm pastry cutter, and place on a baking sheet. Brush with milk to glaze. Bake in the oven for 8–10 minutes, until well risen and golden brown. Transfer to a wire rack to cool.

Makes 12

Note: To give these traditional scones a warm, spicy flavour, add a teaspoon of ground cinnamon to the flour at the start of this recipe. Serve with crème fraîche and strawberries.

Oven temperature 220°C, 425°F, Gas 7

Wensleydale and Apple Scones

60g butter, cubed, plus extra
for greasing

200g self-raising flour

1 teaspoon baking powder

salt

60g fine oatmeal, plus extra
for dusting

1 teaspoon English mustard powder

1 teaspoon light muscovado sugar

125g Wensleydale cheese,
cut into 1cm cubes

1 large or 2 small eating apples,
peeled, cored and chopped
into 5mm pieces

4–5 tablespoons soured cream or
buttermilk, plus extra for glazing

1   Preheat the oven to 200°C. Grease a baking sheet.
2   Sift the flour, baking powder and a good pinch of salt into
    a bowl, then stir in the oatmeal, mustard powder and sugar.
    Rub in the butter using your fingertips until it resembles fine
    breadcrumbs. Stir in the cheese and apples and bind with just
    enough soured cream or buttermilk to make a soft but not sticky
    dough.
3   Roll out the dough on a floured surface to about 2cm thick
    and stamp out 8 scones, using a 6cm pastry cutter. Without
    overhandling the dough, press the trimmings together and roll
    out again to make more scones. Place on the baking sheet,
    brush the tops with soured cream or buttermilk and lightly dust
    with oatmeal. Bake for 15 minutes, then cool on a wire rack
    for a few minutes before serving.

Makes 10 –12

*Wensleydale cheese can be replaced with another crumbly, moist
table cheese such as Pyengana cheddar (Australian), Romney mature
(Australian), Grabetto (Australian), or Barry's bay cheddar (New
Zealand). These scones bring together a blend of sweet and savoury.
Try them with clotted cream.*

Oven temperature 200°C, 400°F, Gas 6

Pumpkin Scones

60g butter
2 tablespoons caster sugar
60g cooked, mashed pumpkin
½ teaspoon nutmeg
1 egg
½ cup milk
360g self-raising flour, sifted

1 Cream butter and sugar together well, add pumpkin and nutmeg and mix well.
2 Add the egg, then mix milk in gradually. Stir in the flour and mix to a soft dough.
3 Turn onto a floured board and knead lightly. Pat out to 2½cm thickness. Cut into rounds with a floured scone cutter.
4 Place the scones onto a greased baking tray, 5mm apart and glaze with milk.
5 Bake in a preheated oven at 210°C for 15–20 minutes. Slide onto a wire cooling rack to cool. Serve with butter.

Makes 12

Oven temperature 210°C, 410°F, Gas 6

Hot-Cross Buns

60g skim milk powder
1 cup warm water
75g sugar
90g margarine, melted
1/2 x 50mg ascorbic acid (Vitamin C) tablet, crushed
14g dried yeast
500g plain flour
1 teaspoon salt
1 teaspoon cinnamon, ground
1 teaspoon mixed spice
1 tablespoon gluten powder
1/2 cup each currants and sultanas
1 tablespoon mixed peel

Cross Batter
3 tablespoons plain flour
3 teaspoons caster sugar
water to mix

Bun Glaze
1/2 cup water
125g granulated sugar

1 Dissolve milk powder in warm water. Add sugar, margarine, ascorbic acid and yeast. Sift the flour, salt, spices and gluten into a large bowl. Pour yeast mixture over dry ingredients, mix well to form a soft dough (add extra warm water if necessary).

2 Knead mixture thoroughly on a floured board for 10 minutes or until smooth.

3 Place dough in a greased bowl, cover with a tea towel and stand in a warm place until mixture doubles in bulk (about 45 minutes). Knead the fruit into the dough. Shape the dough into 16 buns and place then in a well greased deep sided baking dish.

4 Leave the buns in a warm place for a further 15–20 minutes. Pipe crosses on each bun using cross batter. Bake in an oven at 230°C for 15 minutes or until buns sound hollow when tapped underneath. Brush buns with glaze while hot.

Cross Batter

1 Mix together flour and sugar, adding sufficient water to give a cream–like consistency.

Bun Glaze

1 Place water and sugar in a small saucepan, stir over low heat until sugar has dissolved. Simmer for 5 minutes without stirring.

Makes 16

Oven temperature 230°C, 450°F, Gas 8

Blue Cheese and Walnut Damper

315g self-raising flour, sifted
250g blue cheese, crumbled
1 tablespoon snipped fresh chives
1 teaspoon paprika
155g walnuts, chopped
1 cup buttermilk or milk
1 tablespoon walnut or vegetable oil
60g grated Parmesan cheese

1   Place flour, blue cheese, chives, paprika and 125g of walnuts in a bowl and mix to combine.

2   Make a well in the centre of flour mixture, add the milk and oil and mix to form a soft dough.

3   Turn the dough onto a lightly floured surface and knead until smooth. Roll into a large ball, flatten slightly and place on a lightly greased baking tray. Sprinkle with the Parmesan cheese and remaining walnuts and bake for 40 minutes or until damper is cooked.

Note: This loaf tastes wonderful served hot with hearty soups or at room temperature as part of a cheese and fruit platter.

Oven temperature 180°C, 350°F, Gas 4

Easy Berry Bread

375g self-raising flour
1^1/2 teaspoons ground mixed spice
1 teaspoon baking powder
1^1/2 tablespoons sugar
30g butter
170mL water
^{1}/2 cup milk
200g raspberries
1 tablespoon caster sugar
4 teaspoons milk

1 Sift flour, mixed spice and baking powder together into a bowl. Add sugar then, using your fingertips, rub in the butter until the mixture resembles coarse breadcrumbs.

2 Make a well in the centre of the flour mixture and, using a round-ended knife, mix in the water and milk and mix to form a soft dough.

3 Turn the dough onto a floured surface and knead lightly until smooth. Divide the dough into 2 equal portions and flatten each into an 18cm round.

4 Sprinkle raspberries and sugar over the surface of 1 round leaving 2^1/2cm around the edge. Brush the edge with a little milk and place the remaining round on top. Seal edges securely using your fingertips.

5 Place loaf on a greased and lightly floured baking tray. Brush surface of loaf with a little milk and bake for 10 minutes at 220°C. Reduce the oven temperature to 180°C and bake for 20–25 minutes longer or until cooked.

Makes one

Note: Butter absorbs other smells easily, so when keeping it in the refrigerator, ensure it's covered and away from foods such as onions and fish or you'll have a strong-smelling butter that will affect the taste of baked goods.

Oven temperature 220°C, 440°F, Gas 7

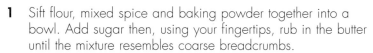

Shortbread

200g butter, softened
100g caster sugar
1 teaspoon vanilla essence
280g flour, sifted
60g rice flour (ground rice), sifted

1 Place butter, sugar and vanilla essence in a bowl and beat until light and fluffy. Add flour and rice flour (ground rice) and mix to combine.

2 Roll out the dough on a lightly floured surface to form a 2cm thick circle.

3 Pinch the edges or press the dough into a large shortbread mould. Place on a lightly greased baking tray and bake for 25 minutes or until lightly browned.

Makes 1

Note: *Butter shortbread originated in Scotland as a festive confection particularly for Christmas and Hogmanay.*

Oven temperature 160°C, 325°F, Gas 3

Cornbread

125g sifted plain flour
4 teaspoons baking powder
¾ teaspoon salt
30g sugar
125g yellow cornmeal
2 eggs
1 cup milk
30g butter, melted
extra butter, to serve

1 Sift flour with baking powder and salt. Stir in the sugar and cornmeal. Add the eggs, milk and melted butter. Beat until just smooth.

2 Pour into a 23 x 23 x 5cm tin lined with baking paper and bake at 220°C in an oven for 20–25 minutes.

3 Remove from the tin and cut into squares. Serve with butter.

Serves 4

Oven temperature 220°C, 425°F, Gas 7

Mini Savoury Croissants

250g prepared puff pastry
1 egg, lightly beaten with
1 tablespoon water
60g Gruyère cheese, grated
4 stalks fresh asparagus, blanched
and finely chopped
¼ teaspoon paprika
freshly ground black pepper

1 To make filling, place cheese, asparagus, paprika and black pepper to taste in a bowl and mix to combine.
2 Roll out pastry to 30mm thick and cut into 10cm wide strips. Cut each strip into triangles with 10cm bases.
3 Place a little filling across the base of each triangle, roll up from the base and mould into a croissant shape. Brush with egg mixture.
4 Place croissants on greased baking trays and bake for 12–15 minutes or until puffed and golden. Serve hot or cold.

Ham and Cheese Croissants

1 Melt 15g butter in a frying pan and cook 100g finely chopped ham and 2 finely chopped spring onions over a medium heat for 3–4 minutes or until onions are soft. Remove from heat, stir in 2 teaspoons finely chopped parsley and black pepper to taste. Cool. Assemble, sprinkling filling with 45g tasty (mature cheddar) cheese and cook as directed.

Chocolate Croissants

1 Chocolate croissants: Use 45g grated milk or dark chocolate to fill triangles. Assemble and cook as directed.

Makes 12

Note: Puff pastry always gives a spectacular result and no more so than in these mini croissants. The secret with these savoury delights is in the shape. Follow the step-by-step instructions to make the quickest and tastiest treats ever.

Cheesy Herb Bread

250g self-raising flour, sifted
1 teaspoon salt
1 teaspoon chicken stock powder
2 tablespoons chopped fresh rosemary
or
1 teaspoon dried rosemary
2 tablespoons chopped fresh dill
2 tablespoons snipped fresh chives
2 tablespoons chopped fresh sage or
1 teaspoon dried sage
185g grated tasty (mature cheddar) cheese
1 egg, lightly beaten
155mL milk
30g butter, melted

1 Place the flour, salt, stock powder, rosemary, dill, chives, sage and 125g of the cheese in a bowl and mix to combine.

2 Combine egg, milk and butter. Add the egg mixture to the dry ingredients and mix to combine.

3 Spoon mixture into a greased and lined 11 x 21cm loaf tin, sprinkle with remaining cheese and bake for 45 minutes or until cooked when tested with a skewer. Turn onto a wire rack to cool.

Makes one 11 x 21cm loaf

Note: Another time, try combining the flavours of thyme, bay leaves and fennel seeds with the rosemary and sage for a loaf infused with the classic 'herbes de Provence'.

Oven temperature 190°C, 370°F, Gas 5

Scones

250g self-raising flour
1 teaspoon baking powder
2 tablespoons sugar
45g butter
1 egg
¹/₂ cup milk

1 Sift together the flour and baking powder into a large bowl. Stir in the sugar, then rub in butter, using your fingertips, until mixture resembles coarse breadcrumbs.

2 Whisk together egg and milk. Make a well in the centre of the flour mixture, pour in the egg mixture and mix to form a soft dough. Turn onto a lightly floured surface and knead lightly.

3 Press dough out to a 2cm thickness, using the palm of your hand. Cut out scones using a floured 5cm cutter. Avoid twisting the cutter, or the scones will rise unevenly.

4 Arrange scones close together on a greased and lightly floured baking tray or in a shallow 20cm round cake tin. Brush with a little milk and bake for 12–15 minutes or until golden.

Makes 12

Note: To grease and flour a cake tin or baking tray, lightly brush with melted butter or margarine, then sprinkle with flour and shake to coat evenly. Invert on a work surface and tap gently to remove excess flour.

Oven temperature 220°C, 425°F, Gas 7

Potato Scones

250g plain flour
1 teaspoon baking powder
1/2 teaspoon salt
125g margarine
1 egg, beaten
50mL milk
125g cold, finely mashed potato
3 shallots, finely chopped
ground black pepper
plain flour, for kneading
butter, for spreading

1 Sift the flour, baking powder and salt together, then rub in the margarine. Beat the eggs and milk together and add to the flour mixture to make a firm dough.

2 Add the potatoes, shallots and pepper. Stir through lightly. Turn onto a floured board or sheet of non-stick oven paper, knead, then roll out to 1cm thickness. Cut into rounds and bake at 230°C in an oven for 15 minutes. Split open while hot and spread with butter to serve.

Serves 6–8

Oven temperature 230°C, 450°F, Gas 8

Cheese and Onion Scones

500g self-raising flour
1 teaspoon salt
¼ teaspoon cayenne pepper
60g margarine or butter
100g grated cheese
1 tablespoon finely chopped parsley
1 tablespoon finely chopped onion
1 egg, beaten
1½ cups milk

1 Sift flour, salt and cayenne. Rub the margarine or butter into the flour. Add cheese, parsley and onion and mix well.

2 Make a well in the centre and add beaten egg and milk all at once, and mix quickly to a soft dough. Turn out on a floured board and knead just enough to make a smooth surface.

3 Roll to 1cm thickness and cut into rounds. Place on a floured tray, glaze tops with milk or beaten egg and milk. Bake at 230°C in an oven for 10–15 minutes or until scones are browned.

Serves 6

Oven temperature 230°C, 450°F, Gas 8

Fresh Herb and Oat Scones

185g self-raising flour, sifted
45g instant oats
$^1/_2$ teaspoon baking powder
30g margarine
2 teaspoons chopped fresh parsley
2 teaspoons chopped fresh basil
2 teaspoons chopped fresh rosemary
190mL skim milk

1   Place flour, oats and baking powder in a bowl. Rub through the margarine until the mixture resembles fine breadcrumbs. Stir in the parsley, basil and rosemary.

2   Make a well in the centre of the mixture and pour in the milk. Mix lightly with a knife until all ingredients are just combined. Turn mixture out onto a lightly floured board and knead lightly.

3   Press dough out evenly to 2cm thickness. Cut into rounds using a 5cm cutter dipped in flour. Arrange scones side by side in a lightly greased 18cm round shallow cake pan. Brush tops with a little extra milk and bake at 220°C for 15–20 minutes or until scones are golden brown.

Makes 9

Make these delicious scones in advance. Freeze and reheat them just before serving.

Oven temperature 220°C, 440°F, Gas 7

Cheese and Bacon Damper

3 tablespoons margarine or butter
310g self-raising flour
2 teaspoons parsley flakes
1 teaspoon chopped chives
125g grated tasty (mature cheddar) cheese
2 rashers cooked bacon, finely chopped
1 egg
185mL milk

1 Rub the margarine or butter into the flour until the mixture resembles coarse breadcrumbs.
2 Stir in the parsley, chives, cheese and bacon, mix well.
3 Combine the egg and milk, stir into the dry ingredients and mix to a soft dough.
4 Turn dough onto a lightly floured board and knead lightly.
5 Shape into a cob, cut a deep cross in the centre and place on a sheet of baking paper on an oven tray.
6 Bake in the oven at 200°C for 30 minutes or until hollow-sounding when tapped underneath.
7 Serve hot with a crock of butter on a buffet table, cut into small pieces.

Serves 6–8

Oven temperature 200°C, 400°F, Gas 6

Olive Soda Bread

125g butter, softened
60g sugar
1 egg
470g wholemeal self-raising flour
185g plain flour
1 1/2 teaspoons bicarbonate of soda
1 1/2 cups buttermilk or milk
125g black olives, chopped
2 teaspoons fennel seeds
1 teaspoon coarse sea salt

1 Place butter, sugar and egg in a food processor and process until smooth. Add wholemeal flour, flour, bicarbonate of soda and milk and process to form a soft dough.
2 Turn the dough onto a lightly floured surface and knead in the olives. Shape the dough into a 20cm round and place on a lightly greased and floured baking tray. Using a sharp knife, cut a cross in the top. Sprinkle with fennel seeds and salt and bake for 45 minutes or until cooked.

Makes one 20cm round loaf

Note: The famous Irish soda bread is influenced here by the Mediterranean flavours of fennel and olives. You can also use one of the many types of marinated olives available.

Oven temperature 200°C, 400°F, Gas 5

Basil-Beer Bread

375g self-raising flour, sifted
60g sugar
6 tablespoons chopped fresh basil
1 teaspoon crushed black peppercorns
1 1/2 cups beer, at room temperature

1 Place flour, sugar, basil, peppercorns and beer in a bowl and mix to make a soft dough.
2 Place dough in a greased and lined 11 x 21cm loaf tin and bake for 50 minutes or until bread is cooked when tested with a skewer.
3 Stand bread in the tin for 5 minutes before turning onto a wire rack to cool. Serve warm or cold.

Makes one 11 x 21cm loaf

Note: This bread is delicious spread with olive or sun-dried tomato paste. Any beer may be used; you can experiment with light and dark ales and even stout to achieve different results.

Oven temperature 160°C, 325°F, Gas 3

Biscuits and Cakes

It's said that cake making is an enviable art. Perhaps in past times it was. These days, cake making is easy, especially when you take the time to look at the wonderful range of mixers, food processors, blenders and other gadgets available to help you obtain professional results every time.

In addition to portable appliances, there is a terrific range of cooking vehicles available – from microwave ovens and counter top stoves to convection oven and an assortment of combination ovens.

Cakes and pastries can be enjoyed at any time, from celebrations and tea parties to just that enjoyable slice with your relaxing 'cuppa'.

In this book we offer a broad range of tasty delights, designed for ease of preparation and positive results, to give you the satisfaction that a home-baked cake or pastry brings.

Cake making can be shared by the whole family. Whether it is stirring a mixture of fruit and eggs for a rich fruit cake kneading a basic bread dough or taking up the challenge of making a more exotic decorative formal cake, all will enjoy the unforgettable fragrance of home baking.

Enjoy the recipes in this book, they are valuable assets to any kitchen library.

Preparing the Cake Tins

- To grease and flour a cake, use a pastry brush lightly brush to cake the tin with melted butter or margarine, then sprinkle with flour and shake to coat evenly. Invert the pan on a work surface and tap it gently to remove excess flour.

To Grease and Line a Round Cake Tin

- Place the cake tin on a large piece of baking paper. Using a pencil, trace around the base, then cut out the shape. Grease the pan and line with paper.

To Line a Deep Cake Tin

- A deep cake tin should be lined on the bottom and sides. Use a double thickness folded strip of baking paper 5cm higher than the cake tin and long enough to fit around the tin and overlap by about $2\frac{1}{2}$cm. Cut out a piece of baking paper to line the base of the tin. On the folded edge turn up about $2\frac{1}{2}$cm and crease, then using scissors snip at regular intervals with scissors across the margin as far as the fold. Grease the cake tin and place the strip inside the tin with the snipped margin lying flat on the base Ensure the ends overlap so that the sides are completely covered by the paper. Place the base piece of baking paper in the tin to cover the snipped margin.

To line a loaf tin

- Cut a strip of non-stick baking paper the width of the base of the loaf tin and long enough to come up the shorter sides of the tin and overlap by $2\frac{1}{2}$cm. When the cake is cooked the unlined sides can be loosened with a knife and the paper ends can be used to lift out the cake.

Baking Secrets

One of the secrets to producing wonderful cakes and biscuits is to understand why certain techniques are used.

Making the Cake

- Many recipes begin by creaming the butter and sugar. This is an important process, as little bubbles of air are trapped in the mixture. It's this air which helps produce a light-textured cake.

- The butter should be softened for the creaming process and the mixture beaten until it's creamy, fluffy and almost doubled in volume.

- Creaming can be done with a balloon whisk, wooden spoon, electric beater or food processor.

- After creaming, egg is often added to the mixture. The egg white forms a layer around each bubble of air and as the cake cooks, the egg white coagulates – forming a wall around each bubble. This prevents the bubbles from bursting and ruining the cake.

- As the cake cooks, the air bubbles expand and the cake rises.

- As the bubbles expand, the gluten in the flour stretches. This continues, until the gluten loses its elasticity.

- Don't open the oven door until at least halfway through the recommended cooking time, or you'll interrupt the rising process. With the sudden drop in temperature, the cake stops expanding and sinks because there's no structure to support it.

- The oven should be preheated to the correct temperature before placing the cake in to cook.

- If baking more than one cake, arrange them so they don't touch each other or the sides of the oven.

- Filling the cake tin is an important step towards a successful result. If your batter is soft, it can be poured into the cake tin, however a firm batter should be spooned into the tin and spread out evenly using a spatula. For light batters, only fill the tin half to two-thirds; heavy batters can fill as much as three-quarters of the tin.

Is the Cake Cooked?

- Test the cake just before the end of the recommended cooking time. To test, insert a skewer into the thickest part of the cake. If it comes out clean, your cake is cooked. If there is cake mixture on the skewer, cook for 5 minutes longer then test again.

- Alternatively, gently press the top of the cake with your fingertips. When cooked, the depression will spring back quickly.

- Another indication that a cake is cooked is that it starts to separate from the side of the pan.

Cooling the Cake

- A freshly-baked cake is very fragile. Allow it to cool for a short time in the tin before turning it onto a wire rack to cool completely.

- Before turning out a cake, loosen the sides with a spatula or palette knife. Then turn the cake onto a wire rack to cool and immediately invert it on to a second wire rack, so that the top of the cake is not marked with lines or indentations from the rack. If you don't have a second wire rack, invert the cake onto a clean cloth on your hand then turn it back onto the wire rack.

Storing Baked Products

- Allow a cake to cool completely before placing it in an airtight container, or condensation will accumulate in the container and cause the cake to go mouldy.

- Keeping times for cakes vary depending on the ingredients used. A fatless sponge only stays fresh for 1–2 days, while one made with fat will keep fresh for 2–3 weeks and heavy, rich fruit cakes will store for a month or more.

- Most undecorated cakes can be frozen. Wrap the cake in freezer wrap or place it in a freezer bag and seal. If you're freezing several cakes, wrap each separately or place freezer wrap or waxed paper between them so they're easy to remove.

- To thaw a frozen cake, leave it in the package and thaw at room temperature. Large cakes take 3–4 hours to thaw, layer cakes 1–2 hours, and smaller cakes about 30 minutes.

Biscuit Barrel

In this chapter you'll find a wonderful array of biscuits and other baked treats. It's easy to understand why they are popular. Not only are they easy to make, they come in a huge variety of flavours and textures. Best of all, they're just the right size for a snack.

Jam Sandwich Biscuits

125g butter
125g icing sugar
1 egg yolk
1 teaspoon vanilla essence
1¾ cups plain flour
3 tablespoons strawberry or raspberry jam
icing sugar for dusting

1. Cream butter and sugar together until light and fluffy. Add the egg yolk and vanilla and beat well.

2. Sift the flour, stir half in to the butter mixture and, when combined add the remainder and mix into a stiff dough. Cover and refrigerate for 10 minutes.

3. Preheat the oven to 180°C. Cut 3 sheets of cooking paper the size of your oven trays.

4. Take half the dough and place on a sheet of cooking paper, cover with a second sheet and roll out the dough to 3mm thick. Remove the top sheet. Slide the cooking paper sheet and biscuit dough onto the oven tray. Stamp circles into the dough with a 6cm fluted cutter, about 5mm apart, in neat rows. Lift off the trimmings in between the rounds. Reusing the top sheet, roll the remaining dough in the same manner. Slide the paper and dough on to the oven tray and stamp out the biscuits as before. Using a fluted cutter, stamp out the centre of each biscuit. Refrigerate for 5–8 minutes then remove the centre and trimmings, place the 2 trays in the preheated oven and cook for 8–10 minutes or until pale straw in colour. Gather the trimming and re-roll as before.

5. Allow the biscuits to cool on the tray. Warm the jam and lightly spread on the underside of the whole biscuit. Sift icing sugar over the top biscuit rings. Sandwich the 2 biscuits together and arrange on a serving platter.

Makes approximately 25

Note: Rolling between cooking paper sheets keeps the trimmings to the same quality as the first rolling as there has not been any extra flour intake.

Date and Orange Oatmeal Biscuits

½ cup light soft brown sugar
½ cup caster sugar
¾ cup sunflower spread
finely grated zest of 1 orange
1 medium egg
1 cup self-raising wholemeal flour
1 cup medium oatmeal
½ cup dried dates, finely chopped

1 Preheat the oven. Line 2 large baking trays with non-stick baking paper. Place the sugars and the sunflower spread in a bowl and beat together until light and fluffy. Add the orange zest, then gradually beat in the egg.

2 Fold in the flour, baking powder and oats, then fold in the dates and mix until well blended.

3 Place heaped teaspoonfuls of the mixture onto the baking trays, spacing well apart to allow the biscuits to spread during baking. Bake in the oven for 15 minutes or until golden brown.

4 Cool slightly on the baking trays, then transfer to a wire rack to cool completely.

Makes 45

Note: Dried dates are a good source of potassium and contain useful amounts of fibre, making them a gentle but effective laxative. Oatmeal also contains soluble fibre and is therefore thought to be helpful in reducing blood cholesterol.

Oven temperature 180°C, 350°F, Gas 4

Fig Pinwheel Biscuits

$^3/_4$ cup butter

$^3/_4$ cup brown sugar

1 egg

$^1/_2$ teaspoon vanilla essence

3 cups plain flour

$^1/_2$ teaspoon bicarbonate soda

$^1/_4$ teaspoon ground cinnamon

$^1/_4$ teaspoon ground nutmeg

2 tablespoons milk

Fig and Almond Filling

1 cup dried figs, finely chopped

$^1/_4$ cup sugar

$^1/_2$ cup water

$^1/_4$ teaspoon ground mixed spice

$^1/_4$ cup blanched almonds,
finely chopped

Fig and Almond Filling

1 Place the figs, sugar, water, and mixed spice in a saucepan and bring to the boil. Reduce the heat and cook, stirring, for 2–3 minutes or until the mixture is thick. Remove the saucepan from the heat and stir in the almonds. Set aside to cool.

Biscuits

1 Place the butter in a bowl and beat until light and fluffy. Gradually add the sugar, beating well after each addition until the mixture is creamy. Beat in the egg and vanilla essence.

2 Sift together the flour, bicarbonate of soda, cinnamon, and nutmeg. Beat the milk and $^1/_2$ the flour mixture into the butter mixture. Stir in the remaining flour mixture. Turn the dough onto a lightly floured surface and knead briefly. Roll it into a ball, wrap it in plastic wrap and refrigerate for 30 minutes.

3 Divide the dough into 2 portions. Roll 1 portion out to a 20 x 25cm rectangle and spread with half the filling. Roll it up like a Swiss roll from the long side. Repeat with the remaining dough and filling. Wrap the rolls in plastic wrap and refrigerate for 15 minutes or until you're ready to cook the biscuits.

4 Cut the rolls into 1cm thick slices. Place the slices on lightly greased baking trays and bake for 10–12 minutes. Stand the biscuits on trays for 1 minute before removing to wire racks to cool completely.

Makes 50

Note: The uncooked rolls can be frozen if you wish. When you have unexpected guests, or the biscuit barrel is empty, these are great standbys.

Oven temperature 180°C, 350°F, Gas 4

Peanut Biscuits (Microwave)

½ cup smooth peanut butter
2 tablespoons butter
¾ cup sugar
1 egg
½ teaspoon vanilla essence
1 cup plain flour
½ teaspoon baking powder

1. Cream the peanut butter, butter and sugar together until light and fluffy. Add the egg and vanilla essence and mix well. Stir the flour and baking powder together and stir into the butter mixture. Mix to a stiff dough and add a little extra flour if necessary.

2. Take 1 rounded teaspoon of the mixture and roll it into a small ball. Repeat with the remainder.

3. Cover the microwave turntable with a sheet of non-stick baking paper cut to size. Place 10 balls around the turntable, 2cm from the edge. Flatten them slightly with the back of a fork. Cook on power level 9 (high) for 2 minutes. Re-press the fork marks left on the biscuits as soon as they're cooked if desired. Slide the paper with the biscuits onto a wire rack and allow to cool before removing from the paper. Cook the remaining biscuits in the same manner.

Makes 25–30

Microwave power level 9 (high)

Pecan Anzacs

¹/₂ cup margarine
1 tablespoon golden syrup
1 teaspoon bicarbonate of soda
2 tablespoons boiling water
1 cup rolled oats
³/₄ cup desiccated coconut
¹/₂ cup plain flour
1 cup sugar
¹/₂ cup chopped pecan nuts

1 Melt the margarine and golden syrup in a saucepan and add the bicarbonate of soda dissolved in the boiling water.

2 Combine the oats, coconut, flour, sugar and pecans. Pour the melted mixture over the dry ingredients and mix well. Place teaspoonfuls of the mixture onto greased oven trays, allowing room for spreading.

3 Bake in an oven for 15 minutes or until golden. Cool the biscuits for a further few minutes on the tray before removing to a wire rack to cool completely. Store in an airtight container.

Makes approximately 48

Oven temperature 180°C, 350°F, Gas 4

Prune and Orange Biscuits

1/2 cup margarine
1/2 cup icing sugar
grated zest of 1 orange
1/2 cup plain flour
3/4 cup pitted prunes, chopped
dark chocolate

1. Cream together the margarine, sugar and orange zest and blend in the flour. Stir the prunes through the mixture.
2. Roll the mixture into small balls and place on a lightly greased oven tray. Flatten with a fork. Bake in an oven for 12–15 minutes.
3. Cool on a tray 5 minutes before removing to a wire rack to cool completely.
4. Decorate the biscuits with melted chocolate.

This recipe makes 4 biscuits

Note: Orange zest may also be peeled off thinly with a potato peeler, then chopped very finely with a large sharp knife

Oven temperature 180°C, 350°F, Gas 4

Coconut Biscuits

½ cup butter, chopped
1 cup brown sugar
1 teaspoon vanilla essence
1 egg
1 cup plain flour
1 cup self-raising flour
1 cup rolled oats
½ cup desiccated coconut
2 teaspoons finely grated lime zest
2 tablespoons lime juice

1 Place the butter, sugar, vanilla essence, egg, flour, self-raising flour, rolled oats, coconut, lime zest and lime juice in a food processor and process until well combined.

2 Drop heaped teaspoons of the mixture onto greased baking trays and bake for 12–15 minutes or until lightly browned. Transfer to wire racks to cool.

Makes 35

Note: The tang of lime and the unique flavour and texture of coconut combine to make these wonderful biscuits.

Oven temperature 180°C, 350°F, Gas 4

Golden Oat Biscuits

1 cup rolled oats
1 cup plain flour, sifted
1 cup desiccated coconut
1 cup sugar
4 teaspoons golden syrup, warmed
½ cup butter, melted
2 tablespoons boiling water
1 teaspoon bicarbonate of soda

1 Place the rolled oats, flour coconut, and sugar in a large bowl. Combine the golden syrup, butter, water and bicarbonate of soda.

2 Pour the syrup mixture into the dry ingredients and mix well to combine. Drop teaspoons of the mixture 3cm apart onto greased baking trays and bake for 10–15 minutes or until the biscuits are just firm. Stand on trays for 3 minutes before transferring to wire racks to cool.

Makes 30

Note: Biscuits should always be stored in an airtight container. Allow the biscuits to cool completely on wire cooling racks before storing.

Oven temperature 180°C, 350°F, Gas 4

Spiced Ginger Drops

125g plain flour, sifted
¼ teaspoon ground ginger
¼ teaspoon ground mixed spice
¼ teaspoon ground cinnamon
½ teaspoon bicarbonate of soda
60g butter, cut into pieces
90g soft brown sugar
2½ tablespoons golden syrup,
warmed
1½ tablespoons finely chopped
glacé ginger or stem ginger
in syrup

1   Place flour, ground ginger, mixed spice, cinnamon and
bicarbonate of soda in a large mixing bowl. Rub in butter
until mixture resembles fine bread crumbs. Stir in sugar, golden
syrup and ginger.

2   Turn onto a lightly floured surface and knead to form
a soft dough. Roll rounded teaspoons of mixture into balls
and place 3cm apart on greased baking trays. Bake for 10–
15 minutes or until golden. Transfer biscuits to wire
racks to cool.

Makes 30

Note: Ginger lovers won't be able to get enough of these spicy cookies.

Oven temperature 180°C, 350°F, Gas 4

Christmas Biscuits

½ cup butter
¾ cup caster sugar
1 egg, lightly beaten
2 teaspoons vanilla essence
¼ cup milk
1 cup plain flour
½ teaspoon bicarbonate of soda
¾ cup roasted hazelnuts, chopped
¾ cup chocolate chips
1 cup shredded coconut
½ cup sultanas
½ cup candied cherries, chopped

1 Place the butter and sugar in a bowl and beat until light and fluffy. Beat in the egg, vanilla essence and milk and continue to beat until well combined.

2 Stir together the flour and bicarbonate of soda and stir into the butter mixture. Add the hazelnuts, chocolate chips, coconut, sultanas and cherries and mix until well combined.

3 Drop tablespoons of the mixture onto greased baking trays and bake for 15 minutes or until golden. Remove to wire racks to cool completely.

Makes 25

Oven temperature 180°C, 350°F, Gas 4

Cinnamon Crisps

½ cup butter
1 cup caster sugar
1 egg
1 cup plain flour
¼ cup self-raising flour
¾ teaspoon bicarbonate of soda
2 teaspoons ground cinnamon

1 Place the butter and ¾ cup of the caster sugar in a bowl and beat until light and fluffy. Add the egg and beat well.

2 Sift together the flour, self-raising flour and bicarbonate of soda and stir into the butter mixture. Turn dough onto a floured surface and knead briefly. Wrap in plastic wrap and refrigerate for 30 minutes or until firm.

3 Place the cinnamon and remaining sugar in a small bowl and mix to combine. Roll the dough into small balls, then roll the balls in the sugar mixture. Place them 5cm apart on lightly greased baking trays and bake for 8 minutes or until golden. Remove to wire racks to cool.

Makes 25

Note: Fat or shortening makes a baked product tender and helps improve its keeping quality. In most baked goods, top-quality margarine and butter are interchangeable.

Oven temperature 180°C, 350°F, Gas 4

Sesame-Pepper Crackers

1 cup rice flour or plain flour, sifted

2 tablespoons sesame seeds, toasted

1 tablespoon chopped fresh sage or 1 teaspoon dried sage

2 teaspoons pink peppercorns, crushed

½ cup mascarpone cheese

¼ cup grated Cheddar cheese

1 egg, lightly beaten

1 Place the flour, sesame seeds, sage and peppercorns in a bowl and mix to combine.

2 Combine cheeses, add to the dry ingredients and mix to form a soft dough.

3 Turn the dough onto a lightly floured surface, knead briefly and roll it into a sausage shape. Wrap in plastic wrap and refrigerate for 40 minutes or until firm.

4 Cut into 1cm thick slices, place on lightly greased baking trays and brush with the egg. Bake for 10 minutes or until the crackers are golden and crisp. Transfer to wire racks to cool.

Makes 30

Note: Mascarpone is made from cream, unsalted and buttery with a fat content of 90 percent. It's mostly used as a dessert cheese, either alone or as an ingredient. If unavailable, mix 1 part thick sour cream with 3 parts lightly whipped double cream, or beat 1 cup of ricotta cheese with 1 cup of light cream until the mixture is smooth and thick.

Oven temperature 190°C, 375°F, Gas 5

Ham-Mustard Scrolls

2 cups self-raising flour, sifted
1 teaspoon baking powder, sifted
¹/₂ cup butter, chopped
1 egg, lightly beaten
¹/₂ cup milk

Ham and Mustard Filling
4 slices smoked ham, chopped
¹/₂ cup ricotta cheese, drained
¹/₂ cup grated Cheddar cheese
2 tablespoons wholegrain mustard

1 Place the flour, baking powder, and butter in a food processor and process until the mixture resembles coarse breadcrumbs. With the machine running, slowly add the egg and milk and process to form a soft dough. Turn the dough onto a lightly floured surface and press out to make a 2cm thick rectangle.

2 To make the filling, place the ham, cheeses and mustard into a bowl and mix to combine. Spread the filling over the dough and roll up from the short side.

3 Using a serrated-edged knife, cut the roll into 2cm thick slices and place on a lightly greased and floured baking tray. Bake for 15–20 minutes or until puffed and golden.

Makes 18

Note: These tangy scone scrolls make an interesting accompaniment to egg dishes at breakfast or brunch. They can also be reheated in the microwave for an afternoon snack.

Oven temperature 220°C, 425°F, Gas 7

Almond Shortbreads

1¾ cups butter (clarified)
¼ cup caster sugar
1 tablespoon vanilla essence
1 cup ground roasted blanched almonds
1 egg yolk
5 cups plain flour
20 cloves
icing sugar, for dusting

1 Preheat the oven.

2 Beat the butter with the caster sugar until pale and creamy, then add the vanilla essence and almonds and mix thoroughly. Add the egg yolk and mix until well combined. Sift the flour and fold it into the mixture with a metal spoon until well combined. Bring the dough together with your hands and knead lightly for 2 minutes until smooth. Wrap in plastic and refrigerate for 15 minutes.

3 Flatten the dough with your hands to 1–2cm thick and roll into half moon shapes. Place a clove in the centre of each cookie and bake on a baking tray for 15 minutes or until golden.

4 Remove from the oven, place on a sheet of baking paper and (while still hot) sift the icing sugar over the shortbreads until well covered. Leave to cool and store them in an airtight container.

Makes 20

Oven temperature 170°C, 340°F, Gas 4

Monte Carlo Biscuits

½ cup butter, softened
1 cup brown sugar
2 teaspoons vanilla essence
1 egg, lightly beaten
1 cup plain flour, sifted
½ cup self-raising flour
1 cup desiccated coconut
1 cup rolled oats
½ cup raspberry jam

Butter Cream
¼ cup butter, softened
½ cup icing sugar
1 teaspoon vanilla essence

Butter Cream

1   Place the butter, icing sugar and vanilla essence in a bowl and beat until light and fluffy.

Biscuits

1   Place the butter, brown sugar and vanilla essence in a bowl and beat until light and fluffy. Add the egg, flour, self-raising flour, coconut and rolled oats, and mix well to combine.

2   Roll tablespoons of the mixture into balls, place them on greased baking trays and flatten slightly with a fork. Bake for 12 minutes or until golden. Transfer to wire racks to cool.

3   Spread half the biscuits with raspberry jam and top with butter cream. Top with the remaining biscuits.

Makes 20

Note: When shaping the biscuits, make sure they're all of uniform size and appearance so that each pair is perfectly matched when sandwiched together.

Oven temperature 190°C, 375°F, Gas 5

Thumbprint Biscuits

¾ cup butter, softened
¼ cup icing sugar, sifted
1 teaspoon vanilla essence
¼ cup plain flour
1 cup self-raising flour
¼ cup custard powder
¼ cup milk
jam, lemon curd or chopped chocolate

1   Place the butter, sugar, and vanilla essence in a bowl, and beat until light and fluffy. Sift together the flour, self-raising flour and custard powder. Fold the flour mixture and the milk, alternately, into the butter mixture.

2   Roll tablespoons of the mixture into balls and place them on a greased baking tray. Make a thumbprint in the centre of each cookie.

3   Fill each thumbprint hole with a teaspoon of jam, lemon curd, or chocolate. Bake for 12 minutes or until biscuits are golden. Transfer to wire racks to cool.

Makes 30

Note: Wrap the dough in plastic wrap and chill for at least 30 minutes to make it easier to shape it into balls. For a subtle toasty nut flavour, roll the balls in sesame seeds before making the thumbprint and filling.

Oven temperature 190°C, 375°F, Gas 5

Afghan Biscuits

3/4 cup butter, softened
1 teaspoon vanilla essence
3/4 cup icing sugar
1 1/2 cups plain flour
1 teaspoon baking powder
1 tablespoon cocoa powder
3 cups cornflakes, crushed
2 tablespoons chopped sultanas
slivered almonds

Chocolate Icing
1 tablespoon butter, softened
1 tablespoon cocoa powder
1 cup icing sugar, sifted
1 tablespoon boiling water

Biscuits

1 Place the butter and vanilla essence in a bowl and beat until light and fluffy. Gradually add the sugar, beating well after each addition until the mixture is creamy.

2 Sift together the flour, baking powder and cocoa powder. Stir the flour mixture into the butter mixture, then fold in the cornflakes and sultanas. Drop heaped teaspoons of the mixture onto greased baking trays and bake for 12–15 minutes. Remove to wire racks to cool completely.

Chocolate Icing

1 Place the butter, cocoa powder, and sugar in a bowl and mix with enough water to make an icing of spreading consistency.

2 Place a little icing on each biscuit and sprinkle with the almonds. Set aside until the icing firms.

Makes 30

Note: Don't store different types of biscuits together as they absorb flavour and moisture from each other.

Oven temperature 200°C, 400°F, Gas 6

Melting Moments

1 cup butter, softened
4 tablespoons icing sugar, sifted
1 cup cornflour
1 cup plain flour

Lemon-Cream Filling
1/4 cup butter, softened
1/2 cup icing sugar
2 teaspoons finely grated lemon zest
1 tablespoon lemon juice

1 Place the butter and icing sugar in a bowl and beat until light and fluffy. Sift together the cornflour and flour, and stir into the butter mixture.

2 Spoon the mixture into a piping bag fitted with a large star nozzle and pipe small rosettes onto greased baking trays, leaving space between each rosette. Bake for 15–20 minutes or until just golden. Allow the biscuits to cool on trays.

Lemon-Cream Filling

1 Place the butter in a bowl and beat until light and fluffy. Gradually add the icing sugar and beat until creamy. Stir in the lemon zest and juice. Sandwich the biscuits together with filling.

Makes 24

Note: Grease the baking trays with a little vegetable oil. Biscuits should be a uniform size; not only will they look more attractive, they'll also cook more evenly.

Oven temperature 180°C, 350°F, Gas 4

Ginger Snaps

1 cup brown sugar
3 teaspoons ground ginger
2 cups plain flour
½ cup butter
1 cup corn syrup
1 teaspoon bicarbonate of soda

1 Sift the sugar, ginger and flour together into a bowl.

2 Place the butter and corn syrup in a saucepan and cook over a low heat, stirring, until the butter melts. Stir in the bicarbonate of soda. Pour the syrup mixture into the dry ingredients and mix until smooth.

3 Drop teaspoons of the mixture onto greased baking trays and bake for 10–12 minutes or until golden. Remove from the oven, loosen the biscuits with a spatula, and allow to cool on trays.

Makes 45

Note: These biscuits become crisp as they cool.

Oven temperature 180°C, 350°F, Gas 4

Almond Cakes

3½ cups blanched almonds
1 cup caster sugar
2 medium eggs
½ cup soft white bread crumbs
⅓ cup honey, warmed to liquid

1   Grind the almonds in a food processor with a little of the sugar. Combine the remaining sugar with the eggs, and whisk until pale, thick, and creamy. Add the ground almonds and the bread crumbs, and stir until well combined.

2   Preheat the oven.

3   Shape (using a tablespoon) roughly into diamond shapes and place on a non-stick baking tray. Bake for 15 minutes.

4   While warm, place the cakes on wire cooling racks and brush with the honey. Allow to cool a little before serving.

Makes 38–40

Note: For easy handling it's best to line the trays with non-stick baking paper.

Oven temperature 180°C, 350°F, Gas 4

Orange-Pistachio Biscotti

2 cups plain flour
1 cup sugar
1 teaspoon baking powder
pinch salt
2 eggs
2 egg whites
1 tablespoon finely grated orange zest
½ teaspoon vanilla essence
½ cup pistachios nuts, shelled

1   Sift together the flour, sugar, baking powder and salt into a bowl.

2   Place the eggs, egg whites, orange zest and vanilla essence in a separate bowl and whisk to combine.

3   Stir the egg mixture and nuts into the flour mixture and mix to make a smooth dough. Turn the dough onto a lightly floured surface and divide into 2 equal portions. Roll each portion into a log with a diameter of 5cm. Flatten the logs slightly and place 10cm apart on a non-stick baking tray. Bake for 30 minutes. Remove from the oven and set aside to cool.

4   Reduce the oven temperature to 150°C.

5   Cut the cooled logs into 1cm thick slices, place the cut sides down onto non-stick baking paper, or trays and bake for 10 minutes or until biscuits are crisp.

6   Biscotti need to be dried out well. Place them in an oven at 75°C for 4 hours. Turn over after 2 hours. Cool on the trays

Makes 48

Oven temperature 180°C, 350°F, Gas 4

Mocha Truffle Biscuits

½ cup butter, chopped

⅔ cup dark chocolate, broken into pieces

2 tablespoons instant espresso coffee powder

2¼ cups plain flour

3 tablespoons cocoa powder

1 teaspoon baking powder

2 eggs, lightly beaten

1 cup sugar

1 cup brown sugar

2 teaspoons vanilla essence

1 cup pecan nuts, chopped

1 Place the butter, chocolate and coffee powder in a heatproof bowl. Set over a saucepan of simmering water and heat, stirring, until the mixture is smooth. Remove the bowl from the pan and set aside to cool slightly.

2 Sift together the flour, cocoa powder and baking powder into a bowl. Add the eggs, sugars, vanilla essence, and chocolate mixture, and mix well to combine. Stir in the pecans.

3 Drop tablespoons of the mixture onto greased baking trays and bake for 12 minutes or until puffed. Stand the biscuits on trays for 2 minutes before transferring to wire racks to cool.

Makes 40

Note: This is the a biscuit version of the traditional rich truffle confection. It tastes delicious as an after-dinner treat with coffee.

Oven temperature 180°C, 350°F, Gas 4

Choc Layer Biscuits

1 cup butter

1 cup brown sugar

¾ cup sugar

2 teaspoons vanilla essence

1 egg

3 cups plain flour

2 teaspoons baking powder

3 tablespoons cocoa powder

3 tablespoons malted milk powder

1 Place the butter, sugars, and vanilla essence in a bowl and beat until light and fluffy. Add the egg and beat well. Sift together the flour and baking powder. Add the flour mixture to the butter mixture and mix to make a soft dough.

2 Divide the dough into 2 equal portions. Knead the cocoa powder into 1 portion and the malted milk powder into the other.

3 Roll out each portion of dough separately on non-stick baking paper to make a 20 x 30cm rectangle. Place the chocolate dough on top of the malt dough and press together.

4 Cut in half lengthwise and place 1 layer of dough on top of the other. You should now have 4 layers of dough in alternating colours. Place the layered dough on a tray, cover with plastic wrap and chill for 1 hour.

5 Cut the dough into 1cm wide fingers and place on greased baking trays. Bake for 15 minutes or until golden and crisp. Transfer to wire racks to cool.

Makes 40

Note: For a special occasion, dip the ends of cooled biscuits into melted white or dark chocolate and place them on a wire rack until the chocolate sets.

Oven temperature 180°C, 350°F, Gas 4

Triple Choc-Chip Biscuits

1 cup caster sugar
½ cup brown sugar
¾ cup vegetable shortening
½ teaspoon vanilla essence
1 egg
2 cups plain flour
1 teaspoon baking powder
½ cup each choc bits, milk bits and white bits

1   Cream together the sugars, shortening and vanilla essence, add the egg and beat in well.

2   Sift the flour and baking powder together and add to the creamed mixture. Stir in the choc bits, milk bits and white bits. Place teaspoonfuls of the mixture onto lightly greased baking trays.

3   Bake in an oven for 15 minutes. Cool on the tray for 5 minutes before removing to a wire tray to cool. Store in an airtight container.

Makes 36

Note: To prevent the biscuits going soft, store them in an airtight tin or plastic container. Biscuits also freeze well, if packed in a plastic bag with the air expelled. They can be kept for up to 6 months in the freezer.

Oven temperature 180°C, 350°F, Gas 4

Night-Sky Biscuits

½ cup butter, softened
1 cup caster sugar
½ teaspoon almond essence
1 egg, lightly beaten
2 cups plain flour
½ teaspoon baking powder
¼ cup milk
½ cup white chocolate, melted
1 cup dark chocolate, melted

1. Place the butter, sugar and almond essence in a bowl and beat until light and fluffy. Gradually beat in the egg.
2. Sift together the flour and baking powder. Fold the flour mixture and the milk, alternately, into the butter mixture and mix to form a soft dough.
3. Roll out the dough onto a lightly floured surface to 5mm thick. Using a star and a moon-shaped cutter, cut out the biscuits. Place them on lightly greased baking trays and bake for 10 minutes or until biscuits are golden and cooked. Transfer to wire racks to cool.
4. Dip the tops of the moon-shaped biscuits in the white chocolate and the tips of the star-shaped biscuits in the dark chocolate. Place on wire racks to set.

Makes 24

Oven temperature 180°C, 350°F, Gas 4

Chocky Road Biscuits

1 cup butter, softened
1 cup brown sugar
2 eggs, lightly beaten
2½ cups plain flour
½ cup cocoa powder
½ cup buttermilk or milk
1 cup white chocolate, roughly chopped
1 cup dry roasted peanuts
1 cup chocolate chips

1 Place the butter and sugar in a bowl and beat until light and fluffy. Gradually beat in the eggs.

2 Sift together the flour and cocoa powder. Add the flour mixture, buttermilk or milk, chocolate, peanuts and chocolate chips to the egg mixture and mix well to combine.

3 Drop tablespoons of the mixture onto lightly greased baking trays and bake for 10 minutes or until cooked. Transfer to wire racks to cool.

Makes 36

Note: Marshmallows, peanuts and chocolate chips must be the three most favourite additions to any cookie designed for kids.

Oven temperature 180°C, 350°F, Gas 4

Crazy Biscuits

½ cup milk chocolate
1 cup butter, softened
1½ cups caster sugar
1¼ cups plain flour
1½ teaspoons baking powder
½ cup freckles (hundreds-and-thousands-coated chocolates)
½ cup caramel whirls

1 Place the chocolate in a heatproof bowl set over a saucepan of simmering water and heat, stirring, until smooth. Remove the bowl from the pan and set aside to cool slightly.

2 Place the butter and sugar in a bowl and beat until light and fluffy. Sift the flour and baking powder together, then add the flour and chocolate to the butter mixture and mix well to combine.

3 Roll tablespoons of the mixture into balls and place on lightly greased baking trays. Flatten slightly and press a freckle or caramel whirl into the centre of each cookie. Bake for 12 minutes or until the biscuits are firm. Cool on a baking tray for 10 minutes, then transfer to a wire cooling rack.

Makes 36

Note: A buttery shortbread-biscuit base is the perfect foil for sweet confectionery decorations.

Oven temperature 180°C, 350°F, Gas 4

Choc-Almond Biscotti

2 cups plain flour
$\frac{1}{2}$ cup cocoa powder
1 teaspoon bicarbonate of soda
$\frac{1}{4}$ cup melted butter
2 tablespoons milk
2 tablespoons dark rum
1 cup sugar
200g blanched almonds
2 eggs
1 egg yolk

1 Sift together the flour, cocoa powder, and bicarbonate of soda into a bowl. Mix in the butter, milk and rum. Make a well in the centre of the flour mixture, add the sugar, almonds and eggs and mix well to form a soft dough.

2 Turn the dough onto a lightly floured surface and knead until smooth. Divide the dough into 4 equal portions. Roll out each portion of dough to make a strip 5mm thick and 4cm wide.

3 Place the strips on a baking tray lined with non-stick baking paper. Brush with the egg yolk and bake for 30 minutes or until lightly browned. Cut the strips into 1cm slices, return to the baking tray, cut-side-down, and bake for 10 minutes longer or until dry.

Makes 35

Oven temperature 180°C, 350°F, Gas 4

Original Choc-Chip Biscuits

1 cup butter, softened
1 cup brown sugar
1 egg
2 cups plain flour
1 1/2 teaspoons baking powder
3 tablespoons desiccated coconut
1 1/2 cups chocolate chips
2 cups hazelnuts, toasted,
roughly chopped

1 Place the butter and sugar in a bowl and beat until light and fluffy. Beat in the egg.
2 Sift the flour and baking powder together, then add the coconut, chocolate chips and hazelnuts to the butter mixture and mix to combine.
3 Drop tablespoons of the mixture onto greased baking trays and bake for 12–15 minutes or until the biscuits are golden. Transfer to wire racks to cool.

Makes 35

Note: This version of everyone's favourite biscuit is full of the flavour of coconut, toasted hazelnuts and a generous portion of chocolate chips!

Oven temperature 180°C, 350°F, Gas 4

Chocolate Sensations

For many, chocolate is a delicious obsession. For the Aztecs, who discovered it, chocolate was 'food for the gods.' In its various forms – powdered, chipped, grated, melted, and chopped – chocolate is one of the most popular ingredients for cakes and bakes.

Simple Chocolate Cake

$^1/4$ cup butter, softened
1 cup sugar
1 teaspoon vanilla essence
2 eggs, lightly beaten
1$^1/4$ cups self-raising flour
3 tablespoons cocoa powder
1 teaspoon bicarbonate of soda
1 cup milk
gold or silver dragees

Chocolate-Butter Icing
$^1/2$ cup dark chocolate
3 tablespoons butter
$^1/4$ cup double cream

Cake

1 Place the butter, sugar, and vanilla essence in a bowl and beat until light and fluffy. Gradually beat in the eggs.

2 Sift the flour, cocoa powder and bicarbonate of soda together into a bowl. Fold the flour mixture and the milk, alternately into the egg mixture.

3 Pour the mixture into a greased and lined 18cm square cake tin and bake for 40 minutes or until the cake is cooked when tested with a skewer. Stand cake in the tin for 5 minutes before turning onto a wire rack to cool.

Chocolate-Butter Icing

1 Place the chocolate, butter and cream in a heatproof bowl set over a saucepan of simmering water. Heat, stirring constantly, until the mixture is smooth. Remove the bowl from the pan and set aside to cool slightly. Spread the top and sides of the cake with the icing and decorate with the dragees.

Serves 8

Oven temperature 180°C, 350°F, Gas 4

Choc-Meringue Cake

Hazelnut Meringue
1 cup hazelnuts, ground
2 tablespoons cornflour
1 1/2 cups caster sugar
6 egg whites

Chocolate Filling
1 cup unsalted butter
1 cup dark chocolate, melted
3 tablespoons caster sugar
2 cups cream
2 tablespoons brandy
1 cup hazelnuts, ground

Chocolate Topping
1 cup bittersweet chocolate
2 teaspoons vegetable oil
whipped cream
strawberries, for decoration

Hazelnut Meringue

1 To make the meringue, mix together hazelnuts, cornflour and 3/4 cup sugar. Beat the egg whites until soft peaks form, add remaining sugar a little at a time and beat until thick and glossy. Fold into the hazelnut mixture.

2 Mark 3 x 10cm squares on baking paper and place them on baking trays. Place the meringue mixture in a piping bag fitted with a small plain nozzle and the pipe mixture to outline squares, then fill the squares with piped lines of mixture. Bake for 40–50 minutes or until crisp and dry.

Chocolate Filling

1 To make filling, beat the butter until soft. Add the chocolate, the sugar and cream and beat until thick. Fold in the brandy and hazelnuts.

Chocolate Topping

1 Place the chocolate and oil in the top of a double saucepan and heat over simmering water, stirring, until the chocolate melts and the mixture is smooth. Remove the top pan and set aside to cool.

Cake

1 To assemble the cake, place a layer of meringue on a serving plate and spread with 1/2 the filling. Top with another meringue layer and the remaining filling. Cut the remaining meringue into squares and position at angles on top of the cake. Drizzle with the topping and decorate with the cream and strawberries.

Serves 10

Oven temperature 120°C, 250°F, Gas 1

Chocolate Pound Cake

³/₄ cup butter, softened
1 ¹/₂ cups caster sugar
3 teaspoons vanilla essence
3 eggs, lightly beaten
1 ¹/₂ cups self-raising flour
¹/₂ cup plain flour
3 tablespoons cocoa powder
1 ¹/₄ cups milk

1 Place butter, sugar, and vanilla essence in a bowl and beat until light and fluffy. Gradually beat in the eggs.

2 Sift together the flours and cocoa powder. Fold the flour mixture and the milk, alternately, into the butter mixture.

3 Pour the mixture into a greased and lined 22cm square cake tin and bake for 55 minutes or until the cake is cooked when tested with a skewer. Stand the cake in the tin for 10 minutes before turning onto a wire rack to cool.

Serves 10

Note: This rich, buttery cake can be served plain, with a ready-made chocolate sauce or with cream. A simple glacé icing drizzled over the top makes another delicious alternative.

Oven temperature 190°C, 375°F, Gas 5

Chocolate Sandwich Cake

125g self-raising flour, sifted
¼ teaspoon bicarbonate of soda
45g cocoa powder, sifted
125g butter, softened
170g caster sugar
2 eggs, lightly beaten
250mL sour cream
125mL double cream, whipped

Chocolate Icing
60g dark chocolate, chopped
30g unsalted butter

Cake

1 Place flour, bicarbonate of soda, cocoa powder, butter, sugar, eggs and sour cream in a large mixing bowl and beat until well combined and mixture is smooth.

2 Spoon batter into two greased and lined 20cm sandwich tins and bake for 25–30 minutes or until cooked when tested with a skewer. Stand cakes in tins for 5 minutes before turning onto a wire rack to cool.

3 Sandwich cold cakes together with whipped cream.

Chocolate Icing

1 Place chocolate and butter in a small saucepan and cook over a low heat, stirring constantly, until melted. Cool slightly then spread over top of cake.

Makes a 20cm sandwich cake, serves 8

Oven temperature 180°C, 350°F, Gas 4

Chocolate-Espresso Cheesecake

250g chocolate wafer biscuits, crushed

$^1/_2$ cup butter, melted

Chocolate-Espresso Filling

2 tablespoons instant espresso coffee powder

1 tablespoon hot water

1 cup cream cheese, softened

1 cup sour cream

3 eggs, lightly beaten

1 cup caster sugar

1 cup dark chocolate, melted

Coffee Liqueur Glaze

4 tablespoons coffee-flavoured liqueur

2 tablespoons dark rum

1$^1/_2$ cups dark chocolate, broken into pieces

$^1/_4$ cup butter

$^1/_2$ cup double cream

Base

1 Place the biscuit crumbs and butter in a bowl and mix to combine. Press the mixture over the base of a lightly greased and lined 25cm springform tin. Refrigerate until firm.

Chocolate-Espresso Filling

1 Place the coffee powder and water in a bowl and mix until the powder dissolves. Set aside to cool slightly.

2 Place the cream cheese, sour cream, eggs, sugar and coffee mixture in a bowl and beat until smooth.

3 Pour $^1/_2$ the filling over the prepared base. Drop 4 tablespoons of melted chocolate into the filling and swirl with a skewer. Repeat with the remaining filling and chocolate and bake for 40 minutes or until the cheesecake is firm. Cool in the tin.

Coffee Liqueur Glaze

1 To make the glaze, place the liqueur and rum into a saucepan and bring to simmering over a medium heat. Simmer, stirring occasionally, until the mixture reduces by half. Add the chocolate, butter and cream and cook, stirring, until the mixture is smooth. Remove the pan from the heat and set aside until the mixture thickens slightly. Spread the glaze over the cheesecake and allow to set.

Serves 10

Oven temperature 200°C, 400°F, Gas 6

Chocolate-Hazelnut Torte

1 1/2 cups dark chocolate,
broken into pieces
6 eggs, separated
1 cup sugar
2 cups hazelnuts, toasted and
roughly chopped
1 tablespoon dark rum
icing sugar, sifted

1   Place the chocolate in a heatproof bowl set over a saucepan of simmering water and heat, stirring, until the chocolate melts. Remove the bowl from the pan and let it cool slightly.

2   Place the egg yolks and sugar in a bowl and beat until thick and pale. Fold the chocolate, hazelnuts and rum into the egg mixture.

3   Place the egg whites into a clean bowl and beat until stiff peaks form. Fold the egg whites into the chocolate mixture. Pour the mixture into a greased and lined 23cm springform tin and bake for 50 minutes or until the cake is cooked when tested with a skewer. Cool the cake in the tin and dust it with icing sugar just prior to serving.

Serves 8

Oven temperature 190°C, 375°F, Gas 5

The Best Chocolate Torte

1 cup dark chocolate, broken into pieces

1 cup brown sugar

$^1/_2$ cup double cream

2 egg yolks

$^3/_4$ cup butter, softened

1 cup sugar

1 teaspoon vanilla essence

2 eggs, lightly beaten

1 cup plain flour

1 cup self-raising flour

$^3/_4$ cup milk

3 egg whites

Rich Chocolate Icing

$^3/_4$ cup sugar

$^3/_4$ cup water

6 egg yolks

1$^1/_2$ cups dark chocolate, melted

1 cup butter, chopped

Decorations

1 cup flaked almonds, toasted

chocolate-drizzled strawberries

Cake

1   Place the chocolate, brown sugar, cream and egg yolks in a heatproof bowl set over a saucepan of simmering water and cook, stirring constantly, until mixture is smooth. Remove the bowl from the pan and set aside to cool slightly.

2   Place the butter, sugar and vanilla essence in a bowl and beat until light and fluffy. Gradually beat in the eggs. Sift together the flours over the butter mixture. Add the chocolate mixture and milk and mix until well combined.

3   Place the egg whites in a clean bowl and beat until stiff peaks form. Fold the egg whites into the chocolate mixture. Pour the mixture into 2 greased and lined 23cm round cake tins and bake for 40 minutes or until the cakes are cooked when tested with a skewer. Stand the cakes in the tins for 5 minutes before turning onto wire racks to cool.

4   To assemble the torte, split each cake horizontally. Place 1 layer of cake on a serving plate and spread with the icing. Top with a second layer of cake and icing. Repeat the layers to use the remaining cake. Spread the top and sides of the cake with the remaining icing. Press the almonds into the sides of the torte and decorate the top with the chocolate-drizzled strawberries.

Rich Chocolate Icing

1   Place the sugar and water in saucepan and heat over a low heat, stirring constantly, until the sugar dissolves. Bring to the boil, then reduce heat and simmer for 4 minutes or until mixture is syrupy.

2   Place the egg yolks in a bowl and beat until thick and pale. Gradually beat in the sugar syrup and melted chocolate. Then gradually beat in the butter and continue beating until the mixture is thick. Cover and refrigerate until the icing is of a spreadable consistency.

Serves 10–12

Note: To prepare the strawberries, wash, pat dry, and place them on a tray. Pipe thin lines of melted dark or white chocolate back and forth across the strawberries and let stand until set.

Oven temperature 180°C, 350°F, Gas 4

Chocolate-Pecan Gâteau

4 eggs, separated

1¼ cups caster sugar

2 tablespoons brandy

2 cups pecan nuts, roughly chopped

2 tablespoons plain flour

Chocolate-Brandy Glaze

2 cups milk chocolate

2 teaspoons instant coffee powder

½ cup double cream

1 tablespoon brandy

1 cup pecan nuts, roughly chopped

Gâteau

1   Place the egg yolks, sugar, and brandy in a bowl and beat until thick and pale. Place the egg whites in a clean bowl and beat until stiff peaks form. Fold the egg whites, pecans and flour into the egg yolk mixture.

2   Pour the mixture into a lightly greased and lined 23cm springform tin and bake for 40 minutes or until the cake is firm. Cool in the tin.

Chocolate-Brandy Glaze

1   Place the chocolate, coffee powder, cream and brandy in a heatproof bowl set over a saucepan of simmering water and heat, stirring, until the mixture is smooth. Remove the bowl from the pan and set aside to cool slightly. Spread the glaze over the top and sides of the cooled cake. Sprinkle the pecans over the top of the cake and press into the side of the cake. Allow to set before serving.

Serves 8

Oven temperature 160°C, 325°F, Gas 3

White Chocolate-Yoghurt Cake

1 cup white chocolate, broken
into pieces
2 cups self-raising flour
1 cup caster sugar
2 eggs, lightly beaten
1 cup plain yoghurt
3 tablespoons butter, melted

White Chocolate Icing
½ cup white chocolate
1 tablespoon double cream

Cake

1 Place the chocolate in a heatproof bowl set over a saucepan of simmering water and heat, stirring, until smooth. Remove the bowl from the pan and cool slightly.

2 Place the flour, sugar, eggs, yoghurt and butter in a bowl and beat for 5 minutes or until the mixture is smooth. Add the melted chocolate and mix well to combine.

3 Pour the mixture into a greased 23cm ring tin and bake for 50 minutes or until the cake is cooked when tested with a skewer. Stand the cake in the tin for 5 minutes before turning onto a wire rack to cool.

White Chocolate Icing

4 Place the chocolate and cream in a heatproof bowl set over a saucepan of simmering water and heat, stirring, until the mixture is smooth. Spread the icing over the top and sides of the cake.

Serves 6–8

Oven temperature 180°C, 350°F, Gas 4

The Best Mud Cake

2¼ cups dark chocolate, broken into pieces
1 cup caster sugar
¾ cup butter, chopped
5 eggs, separated
3 tablespoons plain flour, sifted
cocoa powder, sifted
extra icing sugar, sifted, for dusting

1 Place the chocolate, sugar and butter in a heatproof bowl set over a saucepan of simmering water and heat, stirring, until the mixture is smooth. Remove the bowl and set aside to cool slightly. Beat in the egg yolks one at a time, beating well after each addition. Fold in the flour.

2 Place the egg whites in a clean bowl and beat until stiff peaks form. Fold the egg whites into the chocolate mixture. Pour the mixture into a greased 23cm springform pan and bake for 45 minutes or until the cake is cooked when tested with a skewer. Cool the cake in the pan.

3 Just prior to serving, dust the cake with the cocoa powder and icing sugar.

Serves 10–12

Oven temperature 180°C, 350°F, Gas 4

Devil's Food Cake

¾ cup cocoa powder
1½ cups boiling water
1½ cups unsalted butter, softened
1 teaspoon vanilla essence
2 cups caster sugar
4 eggs
2½ cups plain flour
3 tablespoons cornflour
1 teaspoon bicarbonate of soda
1 teaspoon salt
½ cup double cream, whipped

Chocolate Butter Icing
1 cup butter, softened
1 egg and 2 egg yolks
1 cup icing sugar, sifted
1 cup dark chocolate, melted and cooled

Cake

1   Combine the cocoa powder and water in a small bowl and mix until blended. Set aside to cool. Place the butter and vanilla essence in a large mixing bowl and beat until light and fluffy. Gradually add the sugar, beating well after each addition until the mixture is creamy. Beat in the eggs 1 at a time, beating well after each addition.

2   Sift together the flour, cornflour, bicarbonate of soda and salt into a bowl. Fold the flour mixture and the cocoa mixture alternately into the egg mixture.

3   Divide the batter between 3 greased and lined 23cm sandwich tins and bake for 20–25 minutes or until the cakes are cooked when tested with a skewer. Stand in the tins for 5 minutes before turning onto wire racks to cool completely.

Chocolate Butter Icing

1   Place the butter in a mixing bowl and beat until light and fluffy. Mix in the egg, egg yolks and sugar. Add the chocolate and beat until the icing is thick and creamy. Sandwich the cakes together using the whipped cream then cover the top and sides with the icing.

Serves 12

Oven temperature 180°C, 350°F, Gas 4

Chocolate-Mocha Cake

1 1/4 cups dark chocolate, broken
into small pieces
4 eggs, separated
3/4 cup caster sugar
3/4 cup unsalted butter, softened
and cut into pieces
2 tablespoons strong black coffee
1/2 cup plain flour, sifted

Chocolate Glaze
1 1/4 cups dark chocolate, broken
into small pieces
1/2 cup unsalted butter
2 tablespoons water

1 Place the chocolate in the top of a double saucepan and heat over simmering water for 5 minutes, or until the chocolate melts. Remove the top pan from the heat and stir until smooth. Set aside to cool.

2 Place the egg yolks and sugar in a bowl and beat until pale and fluffy. Add the butter and beat the mixture until creamy. Add the coffee and chocolate and continue beating the mixture until it's creamy. Sift the flour over the mixture and fold in lightly.

3 Beat the egg whites until soft peaks form. Lightly fold the egg-whites into the chocolate mixture. Pour into a greased and lined 20cm round cake tin and bake for 30 minutes, or until firm to the touch. Turn off the oven and cool the cake in the oven with the door ajar. Remove from the tin and refrigerate for 2 hours or overnight.

4 To make the glaze, place the chocolate, butter and water in the top of a double saucepan and heat over simmering water until the chocolate and butter melt. Remove the top pan from the heat and stir the ingredients to combine. Set aside to cool.

5 Remove the cake from the refrigerator and place on a wire rack. Place the rack on a tray and the pour glaze over the cake, smoothing it over the edges and onto the sides with a spatula. Leave until completely set. Transfer the cake to a flat serving platter and cut into slices to serve.

Serves 10

Oven temperature 160°C, 325°F, Gas 3

A Piece of Cake

Whether it be for a tempting snack, a special treat or a formal afternoon tea, a freshly baked cake is the most universally accepted offering. Try cake cut in wedges with cream, or a rich buttery cake served on its own or with a rich chocolate sauce.

Egyptian Torte

1³⁄₄ cups unsalted butter
370g kataifi
sprinkle of pistachio nuts

Cream Filling
1 cup ground rice
1¹⁄₂ cups sour cream
¹⁄₂ cup sugar
2 cups milk

Syrup
1 cup sugar
¹⁄₂ cup water
2 teaspoons lemon juice
1 teaspoon orange water or vanilla

1 Preheat oven. Grease 3 x 23cm cake tins with butter. Divide the kataifi and place ¹⁄₃ in each cake tin. Loosen the tightly packed strands of dough to get rid of any lumps.

2 Melt the butter and pour over the pastry, making sure the kataifi is completely coated.

3 Bake for 45 minutes in a moderate oven. Increase the temperature to 230°C and bake for a further 10 minutes or until golden brown.

4 Meanwhile make cream filling. Combine the ground rice, sour cream and sugar with the milk.

5 Cook over a low heat, whisking constantly, until the mixture is smooth. Continue cooking, still stirring over a low heat, for a further 20 minutes or until thick and ribbony. Set aside to cool.

6 To make the syrup, combine the sugar, water, and lemon juice. Bring to the boil, then the reduce the heat and simmer for 5–7 minutes. Add the orange water or vanilla. The syrup is ready when it coats a wooden spoon. Set aside and cool to lukewarm.

7 When the kataifi is cooked, drain the excess butter from the tins (you may reserve it for other cooking purposes). Pour the syrup onto the kataifi discs while in the tins. Stand for 30 minutes to let it soak.

8 Place the disc on a flat serving platter and spread it with half the cream filling. Top with a second disc, spread with the remainder of the filling and place the third disc on top.

9 Sprinkle the pistachio nuts over the top of cake to garnish.

Serves 12

Note: *Kataifi is a type of shredded filo pastry. You can buy it in Middle Eastern food markets.*

Oven temperature 180°C, 350°F, Gas 4

Almond Cake

1 cup self-raising flour
3/4 cup caster sugar
3 tablespoons ground almonds
1 cup plain yoghurt
1 egg, beaten
1/2 cup safflower oil
1 tablespoon dark rum
1 teaspoon grated lemon zest
whipped cream

For Brushing
1 tablespoon apricot jam
2 teaspoons dark rum

1 Grease a 20cm wide round cake and tin cover the base with non-stick baking paper.

2 Sift together the flour and baking powder. In a bowl, combine them with the sugar and 1/2 the ground almonds.

3 Mix together the yoghurt, egg, oil, rum and lemon zest, and pour onto the flour. Stir until well combined.

4 Pour the mixture into the prepared tin. Sprinkle with the remaining almonds and bake in a preheated oven for 40–45 minutes.

5 Heat together the apricot jam and rum. When the cake is cooked and has cooled a little, brush the mixture thickly over the top of the cake.

6 Serve cut into wedges with the whipped cream.

Serves 4

Oven temperature 200°C, 400°F, Gas 6

Profiteroles

Pastry
1 cup water
4 tablespoons margarine
1 cup plain flour, sifted
3 eggs, beaten

Filling
1 cup double cream
2 tablespoons icing sugar
2 teaspoons coffee liqueur or one tablespoon strong black coffee

Chocolate Sauce
1 1/2 cups dark chocolate
1/4 cup cream

1 Place the water and margarine in a saucepan and cook over a gentle heat until the margarine has melted and the water boils. Remove from the heat, add the sifted flour and stir vigorously. Return to the heat and stir continuously until the mixture forms a ball around the spoon. Cool.

2 Gradually beat in the eggs, beating well after each addition. Place teaspoons of the mixture onto greased oven trays sprinkle with cold water.

3 Bake in a pre-heated oven at 200°C for 10 minutes, reduce heat to 180°C and cook for a further 30 minutes or until the puffs are golden and fall lightly in the hand. Pierce the puffs to allow steam to escape. Cool in a draught-free place.

5 To make the filling, whip the cream to stiff stage, adding icing sugar and coffee liqueur. Fill the profiteroles. To make the chocolate sauce, combine chocolate and cream in a small saucepan and bring to simmer, do not boil. Then spoon chocolate sauce over top of profiteroles to coat..

Makes approximately 20

Oven temperature 180°C, 350°F, Gas 4

Baked Double Cheese Cheesecake

Crumb Crust
2¹/₂ cups sweet biscuit crumbs
¹/₂ cup margarine, melted
2 teaspoons hot water

Filling
1¹/₂ cups cream cheese, softened
1 cup ricotta cheese
³/₄ cup caster sugar
1 teaspoon vanilla essence
3 eggs
1 tablespoon lemon juice

Topping
1 cup sour cream
1 tablespoon caster sugar
3 tablespoons toasted slivered almonds

Crumb Crust

1 To make the crust, combine the biscuit crumbs, margarine and hot water. Mix well.

2 Press the mixture onto the base and half way up the sides of a 23cm springform cake tin. Refrigerate.

Filling

1 Eat the cream cheese until smooth. Blend in the ricotta, sugar, vanilla essence, eggs, and lemon juice. Beat until well combined.

2 Pour the filling into the prepared crust. Bake in a preheated oven for 45 minutes.

Topping

1 To make the topping, combine the sour cream, sugar and almonds. Pour the topping over the filling and bake for a further 20 minutes. Cool in the tin. Refrigerate overnight before cutting.

Serves 10

Oven temperature 150°C, 300°F, Gas 2

Passionfruit Sponge

1 tablespoon butter, plus extra for greasing
3 tablespoons cornflour,
5 eggs, separated
³/₄ cup caster sugar
1 cup self-raising flour
pinch salt
4 tablespoons boiling water
1 cup whipped cream

Passionfruit Butter
pulp of 4 fresh passionfruit or
1 tablespoon canned passionfruit pulp
½ cup sugar
2 eggs
¼ cup butter

Passionfruit Icing
1 tablespoon butter
2 tablespoons icing sugar
juice and pulp of 1 passionfruit

Sponge

1 Grease 2 x 20cm sponge sandwich tins. Cut a circle of greaseproof paper and line the base of each. Grease the paper and dust the tins with the cornflour. Beat the egg whites in a clean dry basin until stiff peaks form. Gradually add the sugar while continuing to beat.

2 Add the egg yolks 1 at a time while beating. Sift the flour, cornflour and salt together. Combine the butter and boiling water and keep ready.

3 Quickly and lightly sprinkle the flour over the egg mixture and fold it in with a large metal spoon. Pour the water and butter around the side of the bowl and continue to fold quickly and lightly. Pour evenly into the 2 prepared tins.

4 Bake in a preheated moderate oven for 20 minutes, or until the tops spring back when lightly touched and the mixture begins to shrink from the sides.

5 Turn out onto a wire rack, remove the paper and cool. Spread 1 cake with passionfruit butter and whipped cream. Spread the passionfruit icing on top of second cake, then sandwich them together.

Passionfruit Butter

1 Place the passionfruit pulp in a bowl. Add the sugar, stir well, and stand for 15 minutes. Place the eggs and butter in the top of a double boiler. Add the passionfruit mixture and stir well. Place over boiling water and stir until the mixture thickens. Cool slightly then bottle in a sterilised jar. Seal when cold. The mixture will thicken on cooling. Use it to fill the sponge cake.

Passionfruit Icing

1 Cream together the butter and icing sugar. Add the passionfruit and mix well. Spread over the cake with a warm knife.

Serves 8

Oven temperature 190°C, 370°F, Gas 5

Chocolate Roll

5 eggs, separated
¼ cup caster sugar
¾ cup dark chocolate, melted and cooled
2 tablespoons plain flour, sifted with 2 tablespoons cocoa powder and ¼ teaspoon baking powder

Chocolate Filling
½ cup dark chocolate
⅔ cup double cream

1 Place the egg yolks and sugar in a mixing bowl and beat until the mixture is thick and creamy. Beat in the chocolate, then fold in the flour mixture.

2 Beat the egg whites until stiff peaks form and fold into the chocolate mixture. Pour into a greased and lined 25 x 30cm Swiss roll tin and bake for 12–15 minutes or until just firm. Turn onto a damp tea towel sprinkled with sugar and roll up from the short end. Set aside to cool.

3 To make the filling, place the chocolate and cream in a small saucepan and cook over a low heat until the chocolate melts and the mixture is well blended. Bring to the boil, remove from the heat and set aside to cool completely. When cold, place in a mixing bowl over ice and beat until thick and creamy.

4 Unroll the cake, spread with the filling and re-roll. To serve, cut into slices.

Serves 8

Note: A chocolate roll filled with chocolate cream makes a special afternoon tea treat or dessert. Irresistibly good to eat, these spectacular cakes are easy to make. Follow these step-by-step instructions for a perfect result every time.

Oven temperature 180°C, 350°F, Gas 4

Raspberry-Cream Gâteau

1 packet vanilla or chocolate
sponge mix
1 cup milk
2 tablespoons Kirsch or Cointreau
liqueur
2½ cups double cream
1½ cups fresh or frozen
raspberries, plus extra for garnish

1 Prepare the sponge mixture according to packet directions for mixing.

2 Cut a piece of greaseproof paper the same size as a 25cm springform tin. Lightly grease the base and sides, place the circle of paper on the base, then grease the paper lightly. Pour the sponge mixture into the tin and cook in the oven for 15–20 minutes, or until the cake springs back when touched. Remove from the oven place on the cake cooler, release spring clip on the tin and remove.

3 When the cake is cool, carefully cut into 4 even rounds. Mix the milk and half the liqueur together and drizzle over the 4 sponge disks. Allow to stand 15–20 minutes.

4 Whip the cream until stiff and add the remaining of the liqueur. Place a sponge layer on a serving plate and spread with a layer of cream and raspberries. Place the second layer on top and repeat until all the layers are used. Cover the top and sides with cream and garnish with the extra raspberries. Chill until ready to serve.

Serves 6

Tip: A squeeze of lemon juice added to double cream makes it whip faster. It's also a great idea to chill the beaters and mixing bowl first.

Variations: Use rum or brandy in place of Kirsch or Cointreau. Layer and cover with chocolate or mocha butter cream and garnish with almonds.

Oven temperature 180°C, 350°F, Gas 4

Lemon-Hazelnut Cake

¾ cup butter, softened
¾ cup caster sugar
1 cup self-raising flour
1 cup ground hazelnuts
3 eggs
¼ cup cream

Lemon Syrup
2 teaspoons grated lemon zest
juice of 2 lemons
½ cup caster sugar

Cake

1. Grease a 25cm fluted tube tin.
2. Place the butter, sugar, flour, hazelnuts, eggs, and cream into a large bowl. Using an electric mixer, beat until smooth, for 2–3 minutes.
3. Pour the mixture into a prepared cake tin and bake in a preheated oven for 40–45 minutes. Turn out onto a wire rack.
4. Place the cake on a cooling rack over a tray. Using a skewer, lightly prick the cake. Pour the hot lemon syrup evenly over the hot cake. Cool and serve with whipped cream if desired.

Lemon Syrup

1. Combine all the ingredients in a saucepan and stir over a low heat until the sugar is dissolved. Bring to the boil, remove from the heat and pour into a jug. Use as directed.

Serves 6–8

Tip: Freeze swirls of fresh cream on a baking tray. When frozen, transfer them carefully to a container for storage. They are ideal for garnishing.

Oven temperature 180°C, 350°F, Gas 4

Strawberry Fruit-Flan

Pastry
1 cup plain flour
2 tablespoons caster sugar
¹/₃ cup margarine
1 egg yolk
1 tablespoon iced water

Filling
1 cup milk
3 egg yolks
3 tablespoons sugar
1¹/₂ tablespoons plain flour
1 teaspoon vanilla essence
1¹/₂ cups strawberries
strawberry jam, warmed

Pastry

1 Place the flour, caster sugar and margarine into the bowl of the food processor. Process until the mixture resembles coarse breadcrumbs.

2 Add the egg yolk and water and mix until the pastry forms a ball around the blade. Remove and knead lightly. Wrap in plastic wrap and refrigerate for 30 minutes.

3 Roll out or press the pastry into a 23cm fluted flan tin with a removable base. Prick the base of the pastry with a fork. Bake in a pre-heated oven for 15 minutes or until golden. Cool.

Filling

1 Heat the milk. Beat together the egg yolks, sugar and flour. Gradually pour the hot milk over the egg mixture while mixing well. Return the custard to the saucepan and stir over low heat until the mixture boils and thickens. Add the vanilla essence. Cover with plastic wrap to stop a skin forming and allow to cool. Spread the custard into the baked pie shell. Decorate with the strawberries and brush them with the jam.

Serves 6-8

Tip: Make your own caster sugar by placing a cup of crystalline sugar into your blender and blend until finely crushed. If you keep blending, the sugar will become pure icing sugar.

Oven temperature 180°C, 350°F, Gas 4

Mocha Walnut Cake

1 packet chocolate buttercake
2 eggs
2 teaspoons instant coffee powder
²/₃ cup water
3 tablespoons margarine
¹/₄ cup chopped walnuts

Coffee Glace Icing
1 teaspoon coffee powder
2 teaspoons of hot water
2 cups sifted icing sugar
1 tablespoon margarine, softened

Cake

1   Make up the cake as directed on the packet. Dissolve the coffee in the water and fold the margarine and walnuts through the cake batter after mixing. Spoon the mixture into a lightly greased 25cm fluted tube tin.

2   Bake in an oven at 180°C for 40 minutes or until cooked when tested. Cool for 5 minutes in the tin before turning out. Cool.

3   Ice with coffee glace icing.

Coffee Glace Icing

1   To make the icing, dissolve the coffee in the water. Blend into the icing sugar and margarine. Mix well.

Serves 6–8

Arabian Date Cake

1 1/4 cups chopped dates
1 cup water
1 teaspoon instant coffee powder
1/2 cup margarine
1/2 cup brown sugar
1/5 cup honey
2 eggs
3/4 cup dark chocolate, melted
2 cups self-raising flour, sifted

1   Combine the dates, water and coffee in a small saucepan. Cook gently until the dates are tender and the liquid has been absorbed.

2   Mash the dates with a fork. Cream together the margarine, sugar and honey until light and creamy. Beat the eggs in, one at a time, beating well between each addition. Add the melted chocolate.

3   Fold in the sifted flour with the date mixture. Mix well. Spoon the mixture into a lightly greased 25cm fluted cake tin. Bake in a pre-heated oven for 45–50 minutes or until cooked when tested.

4   Cool for 5 minutes in the tin. Serve warm or cold spread with margarine or coffee-flavoured cream cheese.

Serves 6–8

Oven temperature 180°C, 350°F, Gas 4

Sicilian Cassata Cake

Sponge
4 eggs
³/₄ cup caster sugar
1 cup self-raising flour, sifted

Filling
2 cups fresh ricotta cheese
³/₄ cup caster sugar
1 cup mixed crystallised fruit, chopped
²/₃ cup dark chocolate, chopped
1 tablespoon chopped pistachio nuts
1 tablespoon Maraschino liqueur

Chocolate Icing
2 cups dark chocolate
¹/₂ cup cream

Sponge

1 Beat the eggs and sugar together with an electric mixer until thick and pale in colour. Fold in the sifted flour and baking powder.

2 Grease a 10 cm cake tin and line the base with greased greaseproof paper cut to fit. Pour in the cake mixture and bake in a pre-heated oven, for 15–20 minutes. Cool completely.

Filling

1 Beat the cheese and sugar together until light and fluffy. Stir in the crystallised fruits, chocolate, nuts and liqueur. Refrigerate. Cut the cake into 2 layers. Place 1 layer in the base of the cake tin in which it was cooked. Fill the centre with the cheese mixture. Cover with a second layer of cake. Refrigerate for 3 hours.

Chocolate Icing

1 Grate the chocolate coarsely and place it in a saucepan. Add the cream and heat very gently until the chocolate has melted. Turn the cake out onto a flat serving dish. Cover the top and sides with the chocolate icing and decorate with chocolate swirls.

Serves 6–8

Oven temperature 200°C, 400°F, Gas 6

Passionfruit Dessert Cake

½ cup margarine
¾ cup caster sugar
grated zest of 1 orange
2 eggs
1¼ cups self-raising flour, sifted
½ cup fresh passionfruit pulp
icing sugar
whipped cream

Passionfruit Sauce
½ cup passionfruit pulp
1 tablespoon icing sugar
1 tablespoon orange juice

Cake

1   Cream together the margarine, sugar and orange zest. Beat in the eggs 1 at a time, beating well between each addition.
2   Fold in the sifted flour along with the passionfruit pulp. Spoon the mixture into a deep, lightly greased 25cm round cake tin. Bake in a pre-heated oven for 40–45 minutes.
3   Serve warm, dusted with sifted icing sugar and accompanied by passionfruit sauce and whipped cream.

Passionfruit Sauce

1   Combine the passionfruit pulp, sugar and orange juice. Serve in a separate bowl.

Serves 6

Tip: Fresh passionfruit may not always be readily available. Canned passionfruit pulp may be used instead. Most canned passionfruit pulp is strained to remove the seeds, but it retains its flavour.

Oven temperature 180°C, 350°F, Gas 4

Crazy Clock Cake

1 packet rainbow cake mix

Frosting
1½ teaspoons margarine
1½ cups icing sugar
1 tablespoon water
1 drop red food colour
½ cup coloured sprinkles chocolate
smarties or M&Ms
licorice strips
coloured dragees

1 Make up the cake as directed on the packet. Spoon the mixture into a lightly greased 23cm round cake tin. Bake in a pre-heated oven for 30 minutes. Cool in the tin for 10 minutes before turning out on a wire rack to cool completely.

2 Make up the frosting as directed. Place the cake on a serving plate. Spread the frosting over the top and sides of the cake.

3 Place a saucepan lid over the centre of the cake. Decorate the remaining rim of the cake with coloured sprinkles. Remove the lid.

4 Place the smarties around the edge of the clock face. Use the dragees to make the numbers and cut the licorice for the clock hands.

Serves 8

Tip: For early attempts at icing, practice on an upturned plate using some butter, icing or mashed potato.

Oven temperature 180°C, 350°F, Gas 4

143

Drum Cake

Cake
8 eggs, separated
1 cup caster sugar
2 teaspoons lemon juice
1 $\frac{1}{4}$ cups plain flour, sifted twice

Butter Cream
2 tablespoons cornflour
1 $\frac{1}{2}$ cups milk
1 egg yolk
2 tablespoons caster sugar
1 cup unsalted butter
$\frac{2}{3}$ cup dark cooking chocolate, melted
1 tablespoon brandy

Toffee Glaze
1 cup sugar
4 tablespoons hot water

Decoration
nuts, finely chopped

1. Cut 8 pieces of non-stick baking paper or greaseproof paper 25cm square. Mark a circle 23cm in diameter on each. If using greaseproof paper, grease the surface with butter. Have ready 2–3 flat baking trays on which to place the paper. Preheat the oven.

2. Place the egg yolks and sugar in a large bowl and beat with an electric mixer until pale and creamy. Add the lemon juice.

3. In a clean basin, stiffly beat the egg whites. Fold in the egg yolk mixture alternately with the sifted flour using a metal spoon.

4. Spread the mixture evenly onto the prepared circles. Bake 2–3 at a time at 220°C for 4–5 minutes or until each sponge is elastic to the touch.

5. Remove with the paper to a wire cooler and quickly cool the remaining discs. Trim the edges with scissors while still warm if necessary. Select the best disc for the top.

6. To make the butter cream, blend the cornflour with a little milk and beat in egg the yolk. Place the remaining milk and sugar into a saucepan and bring to the boil. Pour a little into cornflour and egg mixture while stirring, then pour the egg mixture back into the milk. Stir over a low heat until the custard thickens. Set aside to cool completely. Cream the butter until light and fluffy. Gradually fold in the cold custard, a little at a time, and stir in the melted chocolate. Add the brandy. Chill a little before spreading on the cake.

7. To assemble the sandwich the sponge disks together with the chocolate cream, reserving some for top and side decoration. Place the cake on a flat serving dish and spread the reserved cream on top and around the sides if desired. Sprinkle lightly with the chopped nuts. Pipe a border of butter cream around the top edge with a small star pipe. Arrange the toffee triangles on top. Do not refrigerate the cake as the toffee toppings will spoil. To serve, cut into wedges between the toffee triangles.

8. To make the toffee glaze, place the sugar and water into a saucepan and stir over heat until the sugar dissolves. Boil without stirring until it turns golden and forms a hard ball when a little is dropped into cold water. Pour into a greased 23cm cake tin and mark into triangle sections. When cool, remove and cut the toffee.

Serves 10

Tip 1: When working with egg whites, let them stand for about 1 hour at room temperature before using.

Tip 2: When making hard toffee mixtures, gently remove from the heat and allow to settle for 1–2 minutes before pouring from the saucepan.

Oven temperature 190°C, 370°F, Gas 5

Black Forest Cherry Cake

4 eggs
³⁄₄ cup caster sugar
1¹⁄₂ cups self-raising flour
3 tablespoons cocoa
1 tablespoon butter, melted in 3 tablespoons hot water
3 tablespoons juice from the canned cherries
1 tablespoon Kirsch

Filling
2 cups canned sour black cherries
1 tablespoon caster sugar
2¹⁄₂ tablespoons cornflour or arrowroot, blended
2¹⁄₄ cups double cream
1 tablespoon Kirsch
1 cup chocolate shavings for garnish

Cake

1 Grease 3 x 20cm sandwich cake tins and line the bases with greased greaseproof paper cut to fit.

2 Beat the eggs and sugar together with an electric mixer until very thick and pale in colour.

3 Sift the flour and cocoa together and fold lightly into the egg mixture using a metal spoon. Quickly fold in the melted butter and water.

4 Pour evenly into the prepared tins and bake in a pre-heated oven for 20–25 minutes or until cooked when tested. The cakes should shrink a little from the sides and the centres should spring back when lightly touched. Rest for 2 minutes in the tins, then turn out onto a cake rack. Remove the paper.

5 Mix 2 tablespoons of juice from the cherries with a tablespoon of Kirsch and drizzle over the cakes when cold.

Filling

1 Drain the cherries and remove the pips. Reserve a few cherries to garnish. Place ²⁄₃ cup of the juice in a saucepan, add the sugar and bring to the boil. Stir in the blended cornflour or arrowroot and stir until it thickens. Allow to cool completely, stirring to prevent a skin forming. Stiffly beat the cream, reserve ¹⁄₃ of it, and lightly fold the cold cherry juice, cherries and Kirsch into the remainder.

2 Place 1 cake on a flat serving plate. Spread with filling, 2cm thick. Place the second cake on top and repeat likewise if 3 layers are used. Cover the top and sides of the cake with reserved cream. Press the chocolate shavings around the sides of the cake and garnish the top with the reserved cherries and chocolate shavings.

Serves 8–10

Oven temperature 190°C, 370°F, Gas 5

Orange and Lime Cheesecake

1 cup plain sweet biscuits, crushed
¹/₃ cup butter, melted
desiccated coconut, toasted

Orange and Lime Filling
³/₄ cup cream cheese, softened
2 tablespoons brown sugar
1¹/₂ teaspoon finely grated
orange zest
1¹/₂ teaspoons finely grated
lime zest
3 teaspoons orange juice
3 teaspoons lime juice
1 egg, lightly beaten
¹/₂ cup sweetened condensed milk
2 tablespoons double
cream, whipped

Cake

1　Place the biscuits and butter in a bowl and mix to combine. Press the biscuit mixture over the base and up the sides of a well-greased 23cm flan tin with a removable base. Bake for 5–8 minutes, then cool.

Orange and Lime Filling

1　Place the cream cheese, sugar, orange and lime zests and juices in a bowl and beat until creamy. Beat in the egg, then mix in the condensed milk and fold in the cream.

2　Spoon the filling into the prepared biscuit case and bake for 25–30 minutes or until just firm. Turn the oven off and cool the cheesecake in the oven with the door ajar. Chill before serving. Serve decorated with the toasted coconut.

Serves 8

Oven temperature 180°C, 350°F, Gas 4

Apricot and Sultana Fruit Cake

2 cups dried, apricots, chopped

1 ½ cups sultanas

4 tablespoons orange juice or orange liqueur

1 cup margarine

1 cup caster sugar

grated zest of 2 oranges

grated zest of 1 lemon

4 eggs

1 cup plain flour

½ teaspoon baking powder

1 cup almond meal or ground almonds

1   Combine the apricots, sultanas, and orange juice or liqueur in a bowl and set aside while preparing the cake batter.

2   Cream together the margarine, sugar and orange and lemon zest, until light and creamy. Beat in the eggs, 1 at a time, beating in well between each addition.

3   Sift the flour and baking powder, and fold into the creamed mixture.

4   Fold in the apricot and sultana mixture and almond meal. Spoon the cake batter into a lightly greased paper, lined 23cm round cake tin. Bake in a pre-heated for 1–1 ½ hours or until cooked when tested. Cool in the tin.

Serves 8 – 10

Note: The cake is best left uncut for 1–2 days to allow it to mature.

Oven temperature 160°C, 325°F, Gas 3

Sultana Cake with Caramel Frosting

¾ cup margarine
½ cup caster sugar
½ cup brown sugar
½ cup apricot jam
2 eggs
1½ cups self-raising flour
½ teaspoon nutmeg, ground
1 teaspoon cinnamon, ground
¼ teaspoon cloves, ground
½ cup buttermilk
½ cup chopped pecan nuts
1 cup sultanas

Caramel Frosting
¾ cup margarine
1½ cups brown sugar
5 tablespoon milk
1 teaspoon vanilla essence
3 cups icing sugar, sifted

1 Cream margarine and sugars, blend in the apricot jam and beat until creamy.

2 Add the eggs, one at a time, beating well between each addition. Sift together the flour and spices and fold into the creamed mixture alternately with the buttermilk.

3 Fold in the pecans and sultanas. Spoon the mixture into 2 lightly greased and paper lined 20cm round sandwich tins. Bake in a pre-heated oven for 30–40 minutes or until cooked when tested.

4 Cool for 5 minutes before removing from the tins. Cool completely before filling and coating with the caramel frosting.

Caramel Frosting

5 Place the margarine and sugar into a saucepan and cook over low heat, stirring continuously, until the sugar dissolves. Add the milk and bring to the boil. Remove from the heat and cool to lukewarm. Beat in the vanilla and icing sugar and continue to beat until the frosting is smooth and creamy.

Serves 8–10

Tip: When icing a layer cake, place 2 strips of grease proof paper on the plate to cover it. When you're finished, pull out the paper and the plate will be clean, with no icing drips to clean up.

Oven temperature 200°C, 400°F, Gas 6

Strawberry Shortcake

2 cups self-raising flour
1 teaspoon baking powder
pinch salt
2 tablespoons sugar, extra for sprinkling
$\frac{1}{2}$ cup butter or margarine
$\frac{1}{2}$ cup milk
$\frac{1}{2}$ cup cream
melted butter
2 cups strawberries
4 cups double cream for whipping

1   Sift together the flour and salt. Add the sugar and rub the butter or margarine into the flour. Make a well in the centre and add the milk and cream. Quickly mix to a soft dough.

2   Turn out onto a floured board and lightly knead 5 times only. Pat out $\frac{2}{3}$ of the dough, into a circle $2\frac{1}{2}$cm thick. Trim the edge with a fluted cutter. Pat out the remaining dough into a circle that is smaller in diameter but the same thickness.

3   Place the larger circle on a greased baking tray and brush with the butter. Place the smaller circle on top and brush with the butter or margarine.

4   Bake in a preheated hot oven for 15–20 minutes until golden on the top and bottom. Remove to a wire rack to cool.

5   While still slightly warm, separate the layers. Fill the centre with the whipped cream and strawberries, which have been sprinkled with a little sugar. Place on the top layer and garnish with more cream and strawberries. Serve with extra cream which has been lightly whipped but is still pouring.

Serves 6

Note: Strawberries may be left whole or hulled and sliced.

Oven temperature 220°C, 440°F, Gas 7

Luxury Tiramisu

12 sponge fingers
²/₃ cup strong black coffee
²/₃ cup coffee liqueur, such as
Tia Maria
1 ¼ cups double cream
½ cup mascarpone cheese
½ cup caster sugar
½ cup plain chocolate, grated, plus
shavings to decorate

1   Line the base and sides of a 500g loaf tin with plastic wrap. Lay 4 sponge fingers in the tin. Mix together the coffee and liqueur and pour ¹/₃ of the mixture into the tin. Put the rest of the sponge fingers into a shallow bowl and pour over the remaining coffee mixture.

2   Whip ½ the cream until it forms soft peaks. Fold in the mascarpone and sugar. Spread ½ the mixture over the sponge fingers in the tin. Sprinkle with ½ the grated chocolate.

3   Top with a layer of the soaked sponge fingers, then add the rest of the cream mixture and grated chocolate. Finish with another layer of soaked sponge fingers and refrigerate for 2 hours. Invert the tiramisu onto a plate and remove the plastic wrap. Whip the rest of the cream and spread it over the top and sides. Decorate with the chocolate shavings.

Serves 6

Note: You can serve this classic Italian dessert right away. But it gets even better after it's been in the fridge for an hour or two, as all the flavours soak into the sponge.

Glossary

Acidulated water: water with added acid, such as lemon juice or vinegar, which prevents discolouration of ingredients, particularly fruit or vegetables. The proportion of acid to water is 1 teaspoon per 300mL.

Al dente: Italian cooking term for ingredients that are cooked until tender but still firm to the bite; usually applied to pasta.

Américaine: method of serving seafood, usually lobster and monkfish, in a sauce flavoured with olive oil, aromatic herbs, tomatoes, white wine, fish stock, brandy and tarragon.

Anglaise: cooking style for simple cooked dishes such as boiled vegetables. Assiette anglaise is a plate of cold cooked meats.

Antipasto: Italian for 'before the meal', it denotes an assortment of cold meats, vegetables and cheeses, often marinated, served as an hors d'oeuvre. A typical antipasto might include salami, prosciutto, marinated artichoke hearts, anchovy fillets, olives, tuna fish and provolone cheese.

Au gratin: food sprinkled with breadcrumbs, often covered with cheese sauce and browned until a crisp coating forms.

Bain marie: a saucepan standing in a large pan which is filled with boiling water to keep liquids at simmering point. A double boiler will do the same job.

Balsamic vinegar: a mild, extremely fragrant, wine-based vinegar made in northern Italy. Traditionally, the vinegar is aged for at least seven years in a series of casks made of various woods.

Baste: to moisten food while it is cooking by spooning or brushing on liquid or fat.

Beat: to stir thoroughly and vigorously.

Beurre manie: equal quantities of butter and flour kneaded together and added, a little at a time, to thicken a stew or casserole.

bird: see *paupiette*.

Blanc: a cooking liquid made by adding flour and lemon juice to water in order to keep certain vegetables from discolouring as they cook.

Blanch: to plunge into boiling water and then, in some cases, into cold water. Fruits and nuts are blanched to remove skin easily.

Blanquette: a white stew of lamb, veal or chicken, bound with egg yolks and cream and accompanied by onion and mushrooms.

blend: to mix thoroughly.

Bonne femme: dishes cooked in the traditional French 'housewife' style. Chicken and pork *bonne femme* are garnished with bacon, potatoes and baby onion; fish *bonne femme* with mushrooms in a white-wine sauce.

Bouquet garni: a bunch of herbs, usually consisting of sprigs of parsley, thyme, marjoram, rosemary, a bay leaf, peppercorns and cloves, tied in muslin and used to flavour stews and casseroles.

Braise: to cook whole or large pieces of poultry, game, fish, meat or vegetables in a small amount of wine, stock or other liquid in a closed pot. Often the main ingredient is first browned in fat and then cooked in a low oven or very slowly on top of the stove. Braising suits tough meats and older birds and produces a mellow, rich sauce.

Broil: the American term for grilling food.

Brown: cook in a small amount of fat until brown.

Burghul (also bulgur): a type of cracked wheat, where the kernels are steamed and dried before being crushed.

Buttered: to spread with softened or melted butter.

Butterfly: to slit a piece of food in half horizontally, cutting it almost through so that when opened it resembles butterfly wings. Chops, large prawns and thick fish fillets are often butterflied so that they cook more quickly.

Buttermilk: a tangy, low-fat cultured milk product; its slight acidity makes it an ideal marinade base for poultry.

Calzone: a semicircular pocket of pizza dough, stuffed with meat or vegetables, sealed and baked.

Caramelise: to melt sugar until it is a golden-brown syrup.

Champignons: small mushrooms, usually canned.

Chasseur: French for 'hunter'; a French cooking style in which meat and chicken dishes are cooked with mushrooms, spring onions, white wine and often tomato.

Clarify: to melt butter and drain the oil off the sediment.

Coat: to cover with a thin layer of flour, sugar, nuts, crumbs, poppy or sesame seeds, cinnamon sugar or a few of the ground spices.

Concasser: to chop coarsely, usually tomatoes.

Confit: from the French verb *confire*, meaning to preserve, food that is made into a preserve by cooking very slowly and thoroughly until tender. In the case of meat, such as duck or goose, it is cooked in its own fat, and covered with the fat so that the meat does not come into contact with the air. Vegetables such as onions are good in confit.

Consommé: a clear soup usually made from beef.

Coulis: a thin purée, usually of fresh or cooked fruit or vegetables, which is soft enough to pour (in French *couler* means 'to run'). A coulis may be rough-textured or very smooth.

Court bouillon: the liquid in which fish, poultry or meat is cooked. It usually consists of water with bay leaf, onion, carrots and salt and freshly ground black pepper to taste. Other additives may include wine, vinegar, stock, garlic or spring (green) onions.

Couscous: cereal processed from semolina into pellets, traditionally steamed and served with meat and vegetables in the classic North African stew of the same name.

Cream: to make soft, smooth and creamy by rubbing with the back of a spoon or by beating with a mixer. Usually applied to fat and sugar.

Croutons: small toasted or fried cubes of bread.

Cruciferous vegetables: certain members of the mustard, cabbage and turnip families with cross-shaped flowers and strong aromas and flavours.

Crudités: raw vegetables, cut in slices or sticks to nibble plain or with a dipping sauce, or shredded vegetables tossed as salad with a simple dressing.

Cube: to cut small pieces with six equal sides.

Curdle: to cause milk or sauce to separate into solid and liquid. Example, overcooked egg mixtures.

Daikon radish (also called mooli): a long white Japanese radish.

Dark sesame oil (also called Oriental sesame oil): dark polyunsaturated oil with a low burning point, used for seasoning. Do not replace with lighter sesame oil.

Deglaze: to dissolve congealed cooking juices or glaze on the bottom of a pan by adding a liquid, then scraping and stirring vigorously whilst bringing the liquid to the boil. Juices may be used to make gravy or to add to sauce.

Degrease: to skim grease from the surface of liquid. If possible the liquid should be chilled so the fat solidifies. If not, skim off most of the fat with a large metal spoon, then trail strips of paper towel on the surface of the liquid to remove any remaining globules.

Devilled: a dish or sauce that is highly seasoned with a hot ingredient such as mustard, Worcestershire sauce or cayenne pepper.

Dice: to cut into small cubes.

Dietary fibre: a plant-cell material that is undigested or only partially digested in the human body, but which promotes healthy digestion of other food matter.

Dissolve: mix a dry ingredient with liquid until absorbed.

Dredge: to coat with a dry ingredient, such as flour or sugar.

Drizzle: to pour in a fine thread-like stream over a surface.

Dust: to sprinkle or coat lightly with flour or icing sugar.

Dutch oven: a heavy casserole with a lid usually made from cast iron or pottery.

Emulsion: a mixture of two liquids that are not mutually soluble; for example, oil and water.

Entrée: in Europe, the 'entry' or hors d'oeuvre; in North America entree means the main course.

Fenugreek: a small, slender annual herb of the pea family. The seeds are spice. Ground fenugreek has a strong maple sweetness, spicy but bitter flavour and an aroma of burnt sugar.

Fillet: special cut of beef, lamb, pork or veal; breast of poultry and game; fish cut off the bone lengthwise.

Flake: to break into small pieces with a fork.

Flame: to ignite warmed alcohol over food.

Fold in: a gentle, careful combining of a light or delicate mixture with a heavier mixture, using a metal spoon.

Frenched: when fat and gristle is scraped and cut from meat on a bone, leaving the meaty part virtually fat free.

Fricassé: a dish in which poultry, fish or vegetables are bound together with a white or velouté sauce. In Britain and the United States, the name applies to an old-fashioned dish of chicken in a creamy sauce.

Galangal: A member of the ginger family, commonly known as Laos or Siamese ginger. It has a peppery taste with overtones of ginger.

Galette: sweet or savoury mixture shaped as a flat round.

Ganache: a filling or glaze made of full cream, chocolate, and/or other flavourings, often used to sandwich the layers of gourmet chocolate cakes

Garnish: to decorate food, usually with something edible.

Gastrique: caramelised sugar deglazed with vinegar and used in fruit-flavoured savoury sauces, in such dishes as duck with orange.

Ghee: butter, clarified by boiling. Commonly used in Indian cooking.

Glaze: a thin coating of beaten egg, syrup or aspic which is brushed over pastry, fruits or cooked meats.

Gluten: a protein in flour that is developed when dough is kneaded, making the dough elastic.

Gratin: a dish cooked in the oven or under the grill so that it develops a brown crust. Breadcrumbs or cheese may be sprinkled on top first. Shallow gratin dishes ensure a maximum area of crust.

Grease: to rub or brush lightly with oil or fat.

Infuse: to immerse herbs, spices or other flavourings in hot liquid to flavour it. Infusion takes 2–5 minutes depending on the flavouring. The liquid should be very hot but not boiling.

Jardinière: a garnish of garden vegetables, typically carrots, pickling onions, French beans and turnips.

Joint: to cut poultry, game or small animals into serving pieces by dividing at the joint.

Julienne: to cut food into match-like strips.

Lights: lungs of an animal, used in various meat preparations such as pates and faggots.

Line: to cover the inside of a container with paper, to protect or aid in removing mixture.

Knead: to work dough using heel of hand with a pressing motion, while stretching and folding the dough.

Macerate: to soak food in liquid to soften.

Marinade: a seasoned liquid, usually an oil and acid mixture, in which meats or other foods are soaked to soften and give more flavour.

Marinara: Italian 'sailor's style' cooking that does not apply to any particular combination of ingredients. Marinara tomato sauce for pasta is the most familiar.

Marinate: to let food stand in a marinade to season and tenderise.

Mask: to cover cooked food with sauce.

Melt: to heat until liquified.

Mince: to grind into very small pieces.

Mix: to combine ingredients by stirring.

Monounsaturated fats: one of three types of fats found in foods. It is believed these fats do not raise the level of cholesterol in the blood.

Naan: a slightly leavened bread used in Indian cooking.

Niçoise: a garnish of tomatoes, garlic and black olives; a salad with anchovy, tuna and French beans is typical.

Noisette: small 'nut' of lamb cut from boned loin or rack that is rolled, tied and cut in neat slices. Noisette also means flavoured with hazelnuts, or butter cooked to a nut brown colour.

Non-reactive pan: a cooking pan whose surface does not chemically react with food. Materials used include stainless steel, enamel, glass and some alloys.

Normande: a cooking style for fish, with a garnish of prawn, mussels and mushrooms in a white-wine cream sauce; for poultry and meat, a sauce with cream, calvados and apple.

Olive oil: various grades of oil extracted from olives. Extra virgin olive oil has a full, fruity flavour and the lowest acidity. Virgin olive oil is slightly higher in acidity and lighter in flavour. Pure olive oil is a processed blend of olive oils and has the highest acidity and lightest taste.

Panade: a mixture for binding stuffings and dumplings, notably quenelles (fish rissoles), often of choux pastry or simply breadcrumbs. A panade may also be made of frangipane, puréed potatoes or rice.

Papillote: to cook food in oiled or buttered greaseproof paper or aluminum foil. Also a decorative frill to cover bone ends of chops and poultry drumsticks.

Parboil: to boil or simmer until part cooked (i.e. cooked further than when blanching).

Pare: to cut away outside covering.

Pâté: a paste of meat or seafood used as a spread for toast or crackers.

Paupiette: a thin slice of meat, poultry or fish spread with a savoury stuffing and rolled. In the United States this is also called 'bird' and in Britain an 'olive'.

Peel: to strip away outside covering.

Plump: to soak in liquid or moisten thoroughly until full and round.

Poach: to simmer gently in enough hot liquid to cover, using care to retain shape of food.

Polyunsaturated fat: one of the three types of fats found in food. These exist in large quantities in such vegetable oils as safflower, sunflower, corn and soya bean. These fats lower the level of cholesterol in the blood.

Purée: a smooth paste, usually of vegetables or fruits, made by putting foods through a sieve, food mill or liquefying in a blender or food processor.

Ragout: traditionally a well-seasoned, rich stew containing meat, vegetables and wine. Nowadays, a term applied to any stewed mixture.

Ramekins: small oval or round individual baking dishes.

Reconstitute: to put moisture back into dehydrated foods by soaking in liquid.

Reduce: to cook over a very high heat, uncovered, until the liquid is reduced by evaporation.

Refresh: to cool hot food quickly, either under running water or by plunging it into iced water, to stop it cooking. Particularly for vegetables and occasionally for shellfish.

Rice vinegar: mild, fragrant vinegar that is less sweet than cider vinegar and not as harsh as distilled malt vinegar. Japanese rice vinegar is milder than the Chinese variety.

Roulade: a piece of meat, usually pork or veal, that is spread with stuffing, rolled and often braised or poached. A roulade may also be a sweet or savoury mixture that is baked in a Swiss-roll tin or paper case, filled with a contrasting filling, and rolled.

Roux: A binding for sauces, made with flour and butter or another fatty substance, to which a hot liquid is added. A roux-based sauce may be white, blond or brown, depending on how the butter has been cooked.

Rubbing-in: a method of incorporating fat into flour, by use of fingertips only. Also incorporates air into mixture.

Safflower oil: the vegetable oil that contains the highest proportion of polyunsaturated fats.

Salsa: a juice derived from the main ingredient being cooked, or a sauce added to a dish to enhance its flavour. In Italy the term is often used for pasta sauces; in Mexico the name usually applies to uncooked sauces served as an accompaniment, especially to corn chips.

Saturated fats: one of the three types of fats found in foods. These exist in large quantities in animal products, coconut and palm oils; they raise the level of cholesterol in the blood. As high cholesterol levels may cause heart disease, saturated-fat consumption is recommended to be less than 15 percent of calories provided by the daily diet.

Sauté: to cook or brown in small amount of hot fat.

Scald: to bring just to boiling point, usually for milk. Also to rinse with boiling water.

School prawns: delicious eaten just on their own. Smaller prawn than bay, tiger or king. They have a mild flavour, low oiliness and high moisture content, they make excellent cocktails.

Score: to mark food with cuts, notches or lines to prevent curling or to make food more attractive.

Sear: to brown surface quickly over high heat in hot dish.

Seasoned flour: flour with salt and pepper added.

Sift: to shake a dry, powdered substance through a sieve or sifter to remove any lumps and give lightness.

Simmer: to cook food gently in liquid that bubbles steadily just below boiling point so that the food cooks in even heat without breaking up.

Singe: to quickly flame poultry to remove all traces of feathers after plucking.

Skim: to remove a surface layer (often of impurities and scum) from a liquid with a metal spoon or small ladle.

Slivered: sliced in long, thin pieces, usually refers to nuts, especially almonds.

Souse: to cover food, particularly fish, in wine vinegar and spices and cook slowly; the food is cooled in the same liquid. Sousing gives food a pickled flavour.

Steep: to soak in warm or cold liquid in order to soften food and draw out strong flavours or impurities.

Stir-fry: to cook thin slices of meat and vegetable over a high heat in a small amount of oil, stirring constantly to even cooking in a short time. Traditionally cooked in a wok; however, a heavy-based frying pan may be used.

Stock: the liquid that results from cooking meat, bones and/or vegetables in water to make a base for soups and other recipes. You can substitute stock cubes for fresh bouillon, but those on a reduced sodium diet will need to take note of the salt content on the packet.

Stud: to adorn with; for example, baked ham studded with whole cloves.

Sugo: an Italian sauce made from the liquid or juice extracted from fruit or meat during cooking.

Sweat: to cook sliced or chopped food, usually vegetables, in a little fat and no liquid over very low heat. Foil is pressed on top so that the food steams in its own juices, usually before being added to other dishes.

Thicken: to make a liquid thicker by mixing together arrowroot, cornflour or flour with an equal amount of cold water and pouring it into hot liquid, cooking and stirring until thickened.

Timbale: a creamy mixture of vegetables or meat baked in a mould. French for 'kettledrum'; also denotes a drum-shaped baking dish.

Toss: to gently mix ingredients with two forks or fork and spoon.

Total fat: the individual daily intake of all three fats previously described in this glossary. Nutritionists recommend that fats provide no more than 35 percent of the energy in the diet.

Vine leaves: tender, lightly flavoured leaves of the grapevine, used in ethnic cuisine as wrappers for savoury mixtures. As the leaves are usually packed in brine, they should be well rinsed before use.

Whip: to beat rapidly, incorporate air and produce expansion.

Zest: thin outer layer of citrus fruits containing the aromatic citrus oil. It is usually thinly pared with a vegetable peeler, or grated with a zester or grater to separate it from the bitter white pith underneath.

Weights and Measures

Cooking is not an exact science; one does not require finely calibrated scales, pipettes and scientific equipment to cook, yet the conversion to metric measures in some countries and its interpretations must have intimidated many a good cook.

In the recipes weights are given for ingredients such, as meats, fish, poultry and some vegetables, but in normal cooking a few ounces or grams one way or another will not affect the success of your dish.

Although recipes have been tested using the Australian Standard 250mL cup, 20mL tablespoon and 5mL teaspoon, they will work just as well with the US and Canadian 8fl oz cup, or the UK 300mL cup. We have used graduated cup measures in preference to tablespoon measures so that proportions are always the same. Where tablespoon measures have been given, they are not crucial measures, so using the smaller tablespoon of the US or UK will not affect the recipe's success. At least we all agree on the teaspoon size.

For breads, cakes and pastries, the only area which might cause concern is where eggs are used, as proportions will then vary. If working with a 250mL or 300mL cup, use large eggs (65g/2$\frac{1}{4}$oz), adding a little more liquid to the recipe for 300mL cup measures if it seems necessary. Use the medium-sized eggs (55g/2oz) with 8fl oz cup measure. A graduated set of measuring cups and spoons is recommended, the cups in particular for measuring dry ingredients. Remember to level such ingredients to ensure an accurate quantity.

English Measures

All measurements are similar to Australian with two exceptions: the English cup measures 300mL/10$\frac{1}{2}$ fl oz, whereas the American and Australian cup measure 250mL/8$\frac{3}{4}$fl oz. The English tablespoon (the Australian desserteaspoonoon) measures 14.8mL / $\frac{1}{2}$ fl oz against Australian tablespoon of 20mL/$\frac{3}{4}$fl oz. The Imperial measurement is 20fl oz to the pint, 40fl oz a quart and 160fl oz one gallon.

American Measures

The American reputed pint is 16fl oz, a quart is equal to 32fl oz and the American gallon, 128fl oz. The American tablespoon is equal to 14.8mL/$\frac{1}{2}$ fl oz, the teaspoon is 5mL/$\frac{1}{6}$ fl oz. The cup measure is 250 mL/8$\frac{3}{4}$ fl oz.

Dry Measures

All the measures are level, so when you have filled a cup or spoon, level it off with the edge of a knife. The scale below is the 'cook's equivalent'; it is not an exact conversion of metric to imperial measurement. To calculate the exact metric equivalent yourself, multiply onces x 28.349523 to obtain grams, or divide 28.349523 grams to obtain onces.

Metric grams (g), kilograms (kg)	Imperial ounces (oz), pound (lb)
15g	$\frac{1}{2}$oz
20g	$\frac{1}{3}$oz
30g	1oz
55g	2oz
85g	3oz
115g	4oz/$\frac{1}{4}$ lb
125g	4$\frac{1}{2}$oz
140/145g	5oz
170g	6oz
200g	7oz
225g	8oz/$\frac{1}{2}$ lb
315g	11oz
340g	12oz/$\frac{3}{4}$ lb
370g	13oz
400g	14oz
425g	15oz
455g	16oz/1 lb
1,000g/1kg	35.3oz/2.2 lb
1.5kg	3.33 lb

Oven Temperatures

The Celsius temperatures given here are not exact; they have been rounded off and are given as a guide only. Follow the manufacturer's temperature guide, relating it to oven description given in the recipe. Remember gas ovens are hottest at the top, electric ovens at the bottom and convection-fan forced ovens are usually even throughout. We included Regulo numbers for gas cookers which may assist. To convert °C to °F multiply °C by 9 and divide by 5 then add 32.

	C°	F°	Gas regulo
Very slow	120	250	1
Slow	150	300	2
Moderately slow	160	325	3
Moderate	180	350	4
Moderately hot	190–200	370–400	5–6
Hot	210–220	410–440	6–7
Very hot	230	450	8
Super hot	250–290	475–500	9–10

Cup Measurements

One cup is equal to the following weights.

	Metric	Imperial
Almonds, flaked	85g	3oz
Almonds, slivered, ground	125g	4½oz
Almonds, kernel	155g	5½oz
Apples, dried, chopped	125g	4½oz
Apricots, dried, chopped	190g	6¾oz
Breadcrumbs, packet	125g	4½oz
Breadcrumbs, soft	55g	2oz
Cheese, grated	115g	4oz
Choc bits	155½g	5oz
Coconut, desiccated	90g	3oz
Cornflakes	30g	1oz
Currants	155½g	5oz
Flour	115g	4oz
Fruit, dried (mixed, sultanas etc)	170g	6 oz
Ginger, crystallised, glace	250g	8oz
Honey, treacle, golden syrup	315g	11oz
Mixed peel	225g	8oz
Nuts, chopped	115g	4oz
Prunes, chopped	225g	8oz
Rice, cooked	155g	5½oz
Rice, uncooked	225g	8oz
Rolled oats	90g	3oz
Sesame seeds	115g	4oz
Shortening (butter, margarine)	225g	8oz
Sugar, brown	155g	5½oz
Sugar, granulated or caster	225g	8oz
Sugar, sifted icing	155g	5½oz
Wheatgerm	60g	2oz

Length

Some of us still have trouble converting imperial length to metric. In this scale, measures have been rounded off to the easiest-to-use and most acceptable figures. To obtain the exact metric equivalent in converting inches to centimetres, multiply inches by 2.54 whereby 1 inch equals 25.4 millimetres and 1 millimetre equals 0.03937 inches.

Cake Dish Sizes

Metric	15cm	18cm	20cm	23cm
Imperial	6in	7in	8in	9in

Loaf Dish Sizes

Metric	23 x 12cm	25 x 8cm	28 x 18cm
Imperial	9 x 5in	10 x 3in	11 x 7in

Liquid Measures

Metric millilitres (mL)	Imperial fluid ounce (fl oz)	Cup and Spoon
5mL	⅙ fl oz	1 teaspoon
20mL	⅔ fl oz	1 tablespoon
30mL	1 fl oz	1 tablespoon + 2 teaspoon
55mL	2 fl oz	
63mL	2¼ fl oz	¼ cup
85mL	3 fl oz	
115mL	4 fl oz	
125mL	4½ fl oz	½ cup
150mL	5¼ fl oz	
188mL	6⅔ fl oz	¾ cup
225mL	8 fl oz	
250mL	8¾ fl oz	1 cup
300mL	10½ fl oz	
370mL	13 fl oz	
400mL	14 fl oz	
438mL	15½ fl oz	1¾ cups
455mL	16 fl oz	
500mL	17½ fl oz	2 cups
570mL	0 fl oz	
1 litre	35.3 fl oz	4 cups

Length Measures

Metric millimetres (mm), centimetres (cm)	Imperial inches (in), feet (ft)
5mm, 0.5cm	¼ in
10mm, 1.0cm	½ in
20mm, 2.0cm	¾ in
2.5cm	1in
5 cm	2in
7½ cm	3in
10cm	4in
12½ cm	5in
15cm	6in
18cm	7in
20cm	8in
23cm	9in
25cm	10in
28cm	11in
30cm	12in, 1 foot

Index

Afghan Biscuits	102	Chocolate Nougat Hearts	55
Almond Cake	131	Chocolate Panforte	53
Almond Cakes	104	Chocolate Pecan Fingers	44
Almond Shortbreads	99	Chocolate Pound Cake	118
Apple and Bran Muffins	24	Chocolate Roll	135
Apricot and Sultana Fruit Cake	148	Chocolate Sandwich Cake	119
Apricot Oatbran Muffins	16	Christmas Biscuits	95
Arabian Date Cake	140	Cinnamon Crisps	96
Baked Double Cheese Cheesecake	133	Classic Blueberry Muffins	12
Baklava	49	Coconut Biscuits	92
Banana and Pineapple Muffins	26	Cornbread	67
Banana Choc-Chip Muffins	21	Cornbread Muffins	17
Basil-Beer Bread	76	Crazy Biscuits	110
Blackberry Spice Muffins	22	Crazy Clock Cake	143
Black Forest Cherry Cake	146	Date and Orange Oatmeal Biscuits	87
Blue Cheese and Walnut Damper	63	Devil's Food Cake	126
Brandy Apricot Slice	41	Double-Fudge Blondies	54
Caramel-Walnut Petits Fours	46	Drum Cake	144
Carrot and Sesame Muffins	31	Easy Berry Bread	64
Cheese and Bacon Damper	75	Egyptian Torte	130
Cheese and Bacon Muffins	28	Fig Pinwheel Biscuits	88
Cheese and Onion Scones	73	Fig Scones	58
Cheesy Apple Muffins	18	Fresh Herb and Oat Scones	74
Cheesy Herb Bread	70	Fresh Strawberry Scones	59
Choc-Almond Biscotti	112	Fruit Medley Slice	48
Choc-Meringue Cake	117	Fruit Slice	40
Choc-Rough Muffins	18	Ginger Snaps	103
Chocky Road Biscuits	110	Golden Oat Biscuits	92
Choc Layer Biscuits	106	Ham-Mustard Scrolls	98
Chocolate-Espresso Cheesecake	120	Hot-Cross Buns	62
Chocolate-Hazelnut Torte	121	Hot Brownies with White Chocolate Sauce	38
Chocolate-Mocha Cake	127	Jam Sandwich Biscuits	86
Chocolate-Pecan Gâteau	123	Lamingtons (Microwave)	37

Lemon-Hazelnut Cake	137	Sicilian Cassata Cake	141
Lemon-Poppy Seed Muffins	25	Simple Chocolate Cake	116
Luxury Tiramisu	151	Soda Bread	58
Macadamia Caramel Squares	36	Spiced Apple Muffins	30
Mango Bran Muffins	22	Spiced Ginger Drops	94
Melting Moments	102	Sticky Chocolate and Raspberry Slice	42
Mini Sardine Muffins	14	Sticky Date Muffins	32
Mini Savoury Croissants	68	Strawberry and Chocolate Slice	52
Mocha Truffle Biscuits	106	Strawberry Fruit-Flan	138
Mocha Walnut Cake	139	Strawberry Shortcake	150
Monte Carlo Biscuits	100	Sultana Cake with Caramel Frosting	149
Mushroom Muffins	20	Sultana Oat Slice	45
Night-Sky Biscuits	109	Sweet Corn and Cheese Muffins	12
Oatbran and Fruit Muffins	13	The Best Chocolate Torte	122
Olive Soda Bread	76	The Best Mud Cake	125
Orange-Pistachio Biscotti	105	Thumbprint Biscuits	100
Orange and Blueberry Muffins	26	Triple Choc-Chip Biscuits	108
Orange and Lime Cheesecake	147	Tuna Puffs	15
Original Choc-Chip Biscuits	113	Two-Fruit Crumble Slice	50
Passionfruit Dessert Cake	142	Wensleydale and Apple Scones	60
Passionfruit Sponge	134	White Chocolate-Yoghurt Cake	124
Peanut Biscuits (Microwave)	89		
Pecan Anzacs	90		
Pistachio Truffles	46		
Potato Scones	72		
Potato Sour-Cream Muffins	28		
Profiteroles	132		
Prune and Orange Biscuits	91		
Pumpkin Scones	61		
Raspberry-Cream Gâteau	136		
Scones	71		
Sesame-Pepper Crackers	97		
Shortbread	66